Preparing Early Career Teachers to Thrive

Preparing Early Career Teachers to Thrive

Sustaining Purpose, Navigating Tensions, and Cultivating Self-Care

Kristina Marie Valtierra

Foreword by William Anderson

TEACHERS COLLEGE PRESS
TEACHERS COLLEGE | COLUMBIA UNIVERSITY
NEW YORK AND LONDON

Published by Teachers College Press,® 1234 Amsterdam Avenue, New York, NY 10027

Copyright © 2024 by Teachers College, Columbia University

Cover art by kareemovic2000 (tree branches) and Anisah Mahfudhah Billah (roots), both via the Noun Project.

All rights reserved. No part of this publication may be reproduced or transmitted in any form or by any means, electronic or mechanical, including photocopy, or any information storage and retrieval system, without permission from the publisher. For reprint permission and other subsidiary rights requests, please contact Teachers College Press, Rights Dept.: tcpressrights@tc.columbia .edu

Library of Congress Cataloging-in-Publication Data

Names: Valtierra, Kristina, author.
Title: Preparing early career teachers to thrive : sustaining purpose, navigating tensions, and cultivating self-care / Kristina Marie Valtierra ; foreword by William Anderson.
Description: New York : Teachers College Press, 2024. | Includes bibliographical references and index.
Identifiers: LCCN 2024009251 (print) | LCCN 2024009252 (ebook) | ISBN 9780807786383 (paperback) | ISBN 9780807786390 (hardcover) | ISBN 9780807782736 (epub)
Subjects: LCSH: Teacher turnover—Prevention. | Teachers—Training of. | Teachers—Professional relationships. | Teachers—Job stress. | Teaching—Psychological aspects.
Classification: LCC LB2840.2 .V35 2024 (print) | LCC LB2840.2 (ebook) | DDC 370.71/1—dc23/eng/20240521
LC record available at https://lccn.loc.gov/2024009251
LC ebook record available at https://lccn.loc.gov/2024009252

ISBN 978-0-8077-8638-3 (paper)
ISBN 978-0-8077-8639-0 (hardcover)
ISBN 978-0-8077-8273-6 (ebook)

Printed on acid-free paper
Manufactured in the United States of America

For all the new teachers out there committed to becoming change makers for educational equity and justice. May you thrive in this magical and vital work!

Contents

Foreword *William Anderson*	xi
Acknowledgments	xiii
Introduction	1
About Me	1
How This Book Came About	3
Equitable and Thriving Teachers	3
The Teachers Included in This Book	4
My Social Location and Lens	7
Humanizing the Teaching Profession	7
Humanistic Teacher Development	9
How to Use This Book	10
1. Understanding Burnout to Turn It Around	**13**
Education Reform, Teacher Recruitment, and Retention	15
Teacher Burnout, Disillusionment, and Demoralization	16
Personal Attributes of Thriving Teachers	19
Conditions for Teachers to Thrive	22
A New Paradigm for Preparing and Supporting Early Career Teachers	24
Conclusion: Teaching to Thrive	25

viii

Contents

2. **Sustaining Purpose: Creating an Authentic Teacher Identity** — 27

James Upholds His Purpose Under Pressure — 27

What Motivates Us to Teach? — 29

Supporting Novice Teachers to Discover Purpose and Identity — 32

Infusing Purpose and Practice in Pedagogy — 35

Insights From Preservice and Early Career Teachers — 41

Conclusion: Teacher Identity Formation — 43

3. **Teaching Is Developmental: Promoting Resilience to Traverse the Learning Curve** — 45

Liz's Journey Toward Resilience — 45

Teacher Development — 46

Supporting Preservice and Early Career Teachers: A Developmental Approach — 50

Insights From Preservice and Early Career Teachers — 56

Conclusion: Resilience and the Early Career Teacher Life Cycle — 58

4. **Conflict Is Inevitable: Novice Teacher Agency to Navigate Tension** — 61

Jenna Faces Tension With Her Veteran Colleagues — 61

Conflict at School — 63

Supporting Preservice and Early Career Teachers to Navigate Conflict — 68

Insights From Preservice and Early Career Teachers — 73

Conclusion: Agency and Courage for Dialogue — 76

5. **Teacher Well-Being: Fueling Identity, Resilience, and Agency for Busy New Teachers** — 77

Anna Reclaims a Well-Being Routine — 77

Contents ix

Being Novice, Being Vulnerable	79
What Works	82
Supporting Preservice and Early Career Teachers: Well-Being Habits	83
Insights From Preservice and Early Career Teachers	90
Conclusion: Well-Being as Humanization	92

6. Humanistic Teacher Development: Building Personalized Plans to Thrive — **93**

Jordan Designs a Plan to Flourish	93
Small Habits Lead to Big Results	95
Goals, Systems, and Habits	95
Supporting Preservice and Early Career Teachers: Personalized Plans to Thrive	97
Jordan's Personalized Plan to Thrive	104
Conclusion: Strategizing to Thrive	106

Conclusion: A Call to Support Teachers to Thrive — **109**

Appendix: TTLC Workshop Agenda Template — **113**

References — **115**

Index — **133**

About the Author — **141**

Foreword

Currently and, arguably, historically, we find ourselves at a crossroads in public education. Social media and 24-hour news cycles have added what seems to be more voices on the American public education system than ever before, and more often than not these new voices added to the critiques of K–12 education rarely have anything good to say. We are inundated with stories about schools failing students, children not being ready to function as adults, teacher and administrator ineptitude, and America falling behind its foreign competition. Add in the impacts of a global pandemic, and one could have a recipe for a cynical and nihilistic vision for the future of public education. It is within this backdrop that we are also facing the biggest teacher shortage this country has seen in decades. This is why Kristina Marie Valtierra's *Preparing Early Career Teachers to Thrive* is a breath of much-needed fresh air.

The book arrives at a time when it is most needed to remind people of the "heart work" of teaching. It reminds us how fun, beautiful, satisfying, and rewarding the profession of teaching can be. Between my 15 years in secondary public education and my current role as director of the teacher education program at the University of Denver, I have seen firsthand the challenges and wonders of being a teacher. I remember those early years in the classroom feeling like I was treading water in the ocean, with wave after wave of the complexity of teaching crashing down on me. I remember wishing my teacher preparation program, which I loved, had better prepared me for the reality of teaching. That is why I champion this book. It is exactly what I was missing in my first years in the classroom and beyond, and it also makes clear that the education atmosphere is not as dire as some would like us to believe.

Considering that the average teacher leaves the classroom after only 5 years, there is a critical need for students in teacher preparation programs and early career teachers to consider the topics within this book. Dr. Valtierra positions the humanity of teachers and students at the forefront of the profession, which is, unfortunately, an underrepresented approach. Thankfully, the book makes it abundantly clear that students and teachers are humans who deserve honor, respect, and love like anyone else. And when students and teachers are given the humanity they deserve, they are able to thrive.

The literature focused on teacher preparation is too often all theory without praxis or all praxis without grounding theory. *Preparing Early Career Teachers to Thrive*, however, provides both aspects clearly and authentically. By listening to the voices of practicing teachers, readers can immerse themselves in the very real conditions of teaching while exploring the tangible outcomes of the supports provided in this text. The book challenges educators to be reflective about their practice and about how they show up every day for their students. The reflection Dr. Valtierra invites is critical for both preservice and inservice teachers because it creates space for a pause—a pause to think about what it is you want for your students beyond good grades and high standardized test scores, a pause to think about what you want for yourself as a professional and how this intersects with your desires for your students.

Too often educators come to a book like this looking for a silver bullet that will solve all the problems they are facing. *Preparing Early Career Teachers to Thrive* is not that—nor should it be. Instead of offering a surface-level quick fix, the book opens the door to classrooms, teachers, theories, and methods that must be thoughtfully considered. Dr. Valtierra arranges the text in a way that guides you through the ebbs and flows of learning and developing the teaching skills that ultimately become foundations of one's practice. After all my years in the classroom and now preparing teachers, this book continues to teach me, reminding me that teaching is a *practice*. And no matter how many years I have under my belt, I am still practicing.

Preparing Early Career Teachers to Thrive stands as an example and shepherd to those looking for ways to develop and improve their practice as educators. I am always pleasantly surprised when I come across a text that leaves me saying, this is exactly what we needed. This is that. Enjoy.

—Dr. William Anderson
University of Denver

Acknowledgments

First, thank you to my former education students for being gracious research participants and thought partners on this project. This book would not exist without your insights. I owe special gratitude to my research assistants Doré Young and Aasir Mecca, both aspiring teachers at the time of publishing this book. Thank you, Doré, for taking field notes during the Teach and Thrive Learning Circles, member checking, keeping us organized, and supporting data analysis. Thank you to Aasir for reading drafts and organizing references. Your insights enlightened this project, and I can't wait for you to be in the classroom thriving and changing lives!

Second, thank you to William Anderson for contributing the compelling foreword to this book and for your unwavering commitment to preparing critically conscious teachers. I am also grateful to the Teachers College Press team for your guidance throughout this project, from acquisition to publication. A special note of gratitude to Emily Spangler for your thoughtful developmental edits. Furthermore, a warm thank-you to Tami Parr of Dairy Creek Media for reading drafts and offering insightful feedback. I appreciate your expertise, encouragement, and enthusiasm for this project. Furthermore, I am grateful to the leadership at Colorado College for the course release and research-related resources that have made this project possible.

Most importantly, this book would not exist without my life partner, Micheal. We are a team and this accomplishment is not mine alone—it's ours. Your unwavering support and love inspire me. And thank you to our three boys, Myles, Carter, and Marcus. You mean everything to me.

Preparing Early Career Teachers to Thrive

Introduction

The classroom remains the most radical space of possibility.

—bell hooks

Teaching is one of the most profound and fulfilling professions. Our work is creative, intellectual, hopeful, joyous, and radical. When we thrive as teachers, we love our work, and our commitment and passion are palpable. Plain and simple, teachers can change lives. Yet too many new teachers are experiencing extreme burnout and prematurely giving up on the profession. *Preparing Early Career Teachers to Thrive: Sustaining Purpose, Navigating Tensions, and Cultivating Self-Care* is for educators concerned with ensuring that new teachers flourish in this vital yet complex profession.

If you picked up this book, you might be a teacher educator or mentor dismayed that your investment in future teachers feels futile when up to 50% (Headden, 2014) exit the profession before they have had adequate time to master their craft. You might be picking this book up as an early career teacher yourself, hoping to preserve your passion for this promising profession. This book will validate your concerns and commitment to equipping early career teachers to thrive and provide you with the tools to do so.

ABOUT ME

I am a career-long teacher. For over 25 years, I have filled several roles in education, and I have been fortunate to learn with and from young children, adolescents, and adult learners. Teaching is my lifeline, and I wouldn't trade it for the world. Yet throughout my career, I have witnessed the crisis of early career teacher burnout and turnover from multiple perspectives. Time and time again, I have observed dedicated, talented, and passionate people prematurely exit the profession.

I began my career as an elementary urban classroom teacher in the late 1990s where I experienced the joy of learning with and from young people while simultaneously navigating the pressures of newly implemented top-down No Child Left Behind (NCLB) reform and a toxic school climate. It didn't take long for my mental, physical, and emotional health to suffer. It was an emotional roller coaster, to put it lightly. Like many new teachers, my first year was the most intense. I was overwhelmed and my work felt never-ending. I felt unprepared and unsupported by my inexperienced administration. I felt alone and, as the only 1st-year teacher in my building, I thought I was the only person who didn't "have it together." Despite my relentless stress, I was passionate about my students and deeply dedicated to giving them the high-quality education they deserved. I spent my time away from school telling stories about the cute, smart, and funny things my students said and did. They inspired me. They gave me hope, levity, and a sense of purpose. Ultimately, they kept me going. Despite the challenges I experienced, I stuck with teaching and stayed in my first school for 4 years. Over those first few years, I gained a lot of confidence in myself and my teaching abilities. I was recognized by my school and district for my students' academic achievement and the strong relationships I built with them and their families.

Then, soon after earning my master's degree in literacy, I moved on to an instructional coaching position in an adjacent urban school district where I collaborated with brand-new teachers, teachers approaching retirement, and everyone in between. While my primary role was to help our school adopt a new literacy curriculum, I also mentored brand-new teachers. I empathized with the whirlwind of multiple and often conflicting demands my newly minted colleagues had to juggle. Next, while working on my doctorate, I served as an educational consultant providing professional development for educators all over the United States and Canada. These experiences taught me that the ensuing pressure and burnout affect teachers in all contexts—whether in urban, suburban, or rural communities; or private, independent, or public schools.

I am now an associate professor and chair of the Education Department at Colorado College, a small private liberal arts institution in the western United States. In this role, I have the privilege of supporting our next generation of aspiring urban teachers—talented and passionate people who wish to make a difference in the lives of the diverse youth who occupy our schools. And that's what I hope to contribute to in this book, extending my outreach to prepare promising early career teachers to thrive.

HOW THIS BOOK CAME ABOUT

As a teacher educator, I frequently ask my students why they want to teach. Aspiring teachers commonly remark that they love being with and empowering youth. They are passionate about the profession, were inspired by teachers from their past, and value teaching as a way to contribute to positive social change. Yet once they enter the workforce, new teachers undergo a reality shock as they learn to juggle the multifaceted professional learning curve (Gilad & Alkalay, 2014; Schaefer, 2013) and navigate educational reform efforts that often prioritize standardized test scores (Dunn, 2018) over the altruistic reasons that inspired them to choose to teach (Anderson & Olsen, 2006). Navigating the tensions between one's professional vision and the complex reality of what it takes to be a teacher in contemporary times contributes to early career teacher burnout (Darling-Hammond, 2010; Sulis et al., 2022) and the epidemic of teacher "churn" (Au, 2009; Diamond & Spillane, 2004). In the United States, numerous studies have calculated that between 40% and 50% of novice teachers exit the profession within the first 5 years of teaching (e.g., Headden, 2014; Ingersoll & Smith, 2003; Johnson, Kraft, & Papay, 2012).

Disheartened by the statistical likelihood that half of the aspiring educators I train could fall victim to teacher churn, I have spent the last several years creating and offering a workshop series for preservice teachers and early career alumni called Teach and Thrive Learning Circles (TTLC). TTLCs make the many contradictions new teachers experience between their professional visions and lived realities transparent. Moreover, these workshops aim to respond to early career teachers' experiences and concerns and equip them with tools to push past symptoms of burnout and ultimately thrive. *Preparing Early Career Teachers to Thrive* is an accumulation of firsthand lessons learned from these workshops and a decade of my research on this topic.

EQUITABLE AND THRIVING TEACHERS

I am committed to preparing critically conscious and culturally sustaining educators who thrive. To do this, I ground my work in decades of multicultural education scholarship. Multicultural education is a broad construct that refers to a set of pedagogical strategies and curricular choices intended to honor diverse cultural backgrounds. In the early 1990s, James Banks (1993) proposed multicultural education as a practice that is comprehensively embedded in school culture, curriculum, and pedagogy. Since then, scholars have helped educators put multicultural teaching into practice through the frameworks of culturally relevant teaching (CRT) (Ladson-Billings, 1995), culturally responsive pedagogy (CRP) (Gay, 2010, 2014), and more recently, culturally sustaining pedagogy (CSP) (Paris & Alim, 2017). Since CSP builds off CRT and CRP, I will use the concept of CSP moving forward in this book.

Too often, schools are places that eradicate culturally and linguistically diverse (CLD) students' cultural ways of being to encourage assimilation. In contrast, teachers committed to CSP affirm student backgrounds, connecting to their prior experiences and cultural frameworks, and creating classrooms in which the cultural frameworks of CLD students are embraced and sustained (Paris & Alim, 2017). Along with methods coursework and intentional opportunities to apply CSP methods, preparing culturally sustaining teachers requires emphasizing and cultivating candidates' critical consciousness and praxis. In tandem, I have found that culturally sustaining preservice and early career teachers benefit from explicit support to flourish. It is only when they are equipped to flourish that they can fully deliver CSP.

THE TEACHERS INCLUDED IN THIS BOOK

Over 50 of my former students have participated in the TTLCs. Over the years, I have accumulated their thoughts, recommendations, reflections on the TTLCs, and aspirations as new teachers. In addition, I followed some of them during their early years in the classroom. This book is based on my accumulation of field notes, interviews, focus groups, questionnaires, and written reflections collected from my workshop participants. While themes from several years of my research have led up to this book, quotes, short anecdotes, and teacher reflections shared throughout this book come directly from one cohort of 22 who participated in the TTLC workshops virtually while they were teaching across the United States. These inspiring novice teachers ranged from preservice to 3rd-year teachers who were teaching in several general education disciplines, in a range of elementary, middle, and high school settings, and were primarily in urban schools. Moreover, the demographics of teachers featured in this book are moderately

Introduction

more diverse than national public school teacher demographics (National Center for Education Statistics [NCES], 2021), with over 30% teachers of color and 20% males (Valtierra, 2022).

Featured participants included six preservice teachers who were full-time student teaching during the workshops.

There were four 1st-year teacher participants, with the majority teaching in elementary school settings.

The largest group of participants were 2nd-year teachers who were serving in a variety of contexts, grade levels, and subject areas.

Finally, four 3rd-year teachers also participated. Each participant, regardless of their years of teaching experience, earned their initial licensure through the same teacher preparation program.

These novice teachers agreed to have a research assistant take detailed field notes of each TTLC session; for me to use their written reflections, work samples, and interviews for this book; and to follow up with them on a routine basis. Furthermore, since the

Table I.1. Preservice Teachers

Name	Gender Identity	Race & Ethnicity	Teaching Context	Subject(s)
Casey	nonbinary	Mixed-race	Urban HS	ELA
Nikki	female	White	Urban HS	Social Studies
Maria	female	Latinx	Urban EL	All Core
Jeffrey	male	White	Urban HS	Social Studies
Carter	male	White	Urban EL	All Core
Jasmine	female	Latinx	Urban EL	All Core

Note. All names are pseudonyms. EL = elementary, MS = middle school, HS = high school, ELA = English Language Arts.

Table I.2. 1st-Year Teachers

Name	Gender Identity	Race & Ethnicity	Teaching Context	Subject(s)
Maria	female	Mixed-race	Urban EL	All Core
Denise	female	White	Urban HS	ELA
Catherine	female	Latinx	Urban EL	All Core
Jordan	male	Asian	Urban EL	All Core

Note. All names are pseudonyms. EL = elementary, MS = middle school, HS = high school, ELA = English Language Arts.

Table I.3. 2nd-Year Teachers

Name	Gender Identity	Race & Ethnicity	Teaching Context	Subject(s)
James	male	White	Urban HS	ELA
Delia	female	White	Urban HS	Math
Mary	female	White	Suburban MS	ELA
Layla	female	White	Urban HS	ELA
Sara	female	Asian	Suburban MS	Science
Summer	female	White	Suburban EL	All Core
Anna	female	Black	Urban MS	Social Studies
Mike	male	White	Urban MS	Science

Note. All names are pseudonyms. EL = elementary, MS = middle school, HS = high school, ELA = English Language Arts.

Table I.4. 3rd-Year Teachers

Name	Gender Identity	Race & Ethnicity	Teaching Context	Subject(s)
Katherine	female	White	Rural EL	All Core
Aubrey	female	White	Urban MS	ELA
Liz	female	White	Urban EL	All Core
Lexie	female	White	Urban EL	All Core

Note. All names are pseudonyms. EL = elementary, MS = middle school, HS = high school, ELA = English Language Arts

practicing teacher participants were members of earlier versions of the TTLCs, we saw this as a fruitful opportunity to co-construct an updated version of the workshops. The newest version encompasses the topics featured in this book—issues that the participating novice teachers felt still resonated with them from their teacher preparation TTLC workshops and specific attention to their real-time experiences and concerns as early career educators. As a bonus, the preservice teachers in the group gained practical insights, inspiration, and informal mentorship from their more experienced peers. While lessons learned from the TTLC workshops inspired much of its content, this book offers comprehensive tools for use in a variety of formats.

MY SOCIAL LOCATION AND LENS

As the author, an educator who has experienced teacher burnout, and the researcher for this book, I am also a participant in the stories this book will tell. Hence, it is crucial to acknowledge my social location and therefore the epistemological lens that I am looking through. I am a white, cisgender, U.S.-born, heritage English-speaking, middle-aged woman. My positionality, in tandem with my experiences in the field of education, informs how I make sense of education and the problems of early career teacher attrition addressed in this book. It is vital to acknowledge that my social location affords me several unearned privileges. And as a person dedicated to social justice, my positionality requires that I prioritize critical consciousness and praxis. I am committed to persistent critical analysis of my interpretations of the world, and in this case, how I make sense of the research shared in this book. I feel a lifelong responsibility to unravel my privileged socialization. At this stage in my development, I identify as a "white transformationalist" (p. 2), which, according to whiteness scholar and educator Gary Howard (2007), entails:

- embracing and seeking difference in one's personal and professional lives;
- embracing a nuanced understanding of how racism and other forms of systemic oppression operate;
- active commitment to dismantling white superiority in schools and society;
- a healthy white racial identity; and
- authentic relationships across differences.

HUMANIZING THE TEACHING PROFESSION

I am writing this book during a period that will undoubtedly make its way into history books. We have collectively faced, and will continue to encounter the effects of, what some call dual and interconnected pandemics: COVID-19 and brutal police murders of innocent Black and Brown people. Both COVID-19 and systemic racism have taken countless lives, wounded the spirits of survivors, and amplified the many social injustices that existed long before the pandemics took root. In their schools and communities, students have been stripped of social support, a sense of belonging, and academic opportunity while navigating illness and loss of loved ones, the stress of potentially being infected by a deadly virus, fears of police brutality, and much more. Moreover, the closing of in-person schools during the pandemic left teachers scrambling to create online learning environments with little resources, training, or recognition of the trauma these pandemics perpetrated on their lives. And while schools are currently back in operation, teachers are still left navigating student learning loss, trauma, and poor mental health, while simultaneously attempting to attend to their personal well-being. The traumas induced by these dual pandemics have disproportionally affected BIPOC, disabled, and low-income teachers and their students (Endo, 2021; Jones, 2021).

Many educators and activists contend that "back to normal" is not good enough and that now is the time to rebuild society and education as we know it. While the problems of teacher burnout and turnover were significant before 2020, we are now in crisis mode, with many previously thriving educators calling it quits and prospective teachers changing course (National Education Association [NEA], 2022). There are daily reports of practicing teachers exiting in droves because they are exhausted, feel demoralized, disrespected, and like our current education system has sucked the joy out of teaching (e.g., Kamenetz, 2022; Ley, 2022; Will, 2022). Now is the time to rethink how we prepare and nourish new educators who are still giving the profession a chance despite some of the grim realities of what it can mean to teach in contemporary times.

At this moment in history, we have an opportunity to abolish antiquated practices (Love, 2020) and humanize education, including how we prepare and support new teachers. While the scope of this book will not solve systemic educational change, I do hope that it contributes to rehumanizing teachers and, concomitantly, how we prepare and support them.

Traditionally, the scholarship on humanistic learning theory focuses on practices that attend to the self-actualization needs (Crain, 2015) of the "whole" child. Such methods include offering choice, prioritizing self-evaluation, making school engaging to increase motivation, recognizing that knowledge and feelings go hand in hand, and creating emotionally and physically safe learning environments for youth to thrive (Duchesne & McMaugh, 2015; Khatib et al., 2013; Maslow, 1968).

Some scholars have argued that humanistic learning theory and the tenets of multicultural education are complementary in preparing

Introduction

teachers to serve systemically marginalized communities (e.g., Alifah, 2018; Allen, 2000). For instance, Allen (2000) studied the merging of humanistic learning theory with multicultural education in a course for predominantly white preservice teachers. He found positive changes in his participants' attitudes and commitments toward meeting the needs of diverse youth.

In many parts of the United States, the racial makeup of public schools has shifted so that non-white students are the majority (NCES, 2019). While equity should always be a central tenet in every school, now more than ever it is imperative that all teachers be prepared and deeply committed to humanize all students, embracing those most vulnerable to systemic racism, ableism, and other forms of discrimination. Moreover, given that minoritized teachers are more susceptible to burnout and attrition (Mahatmya et al., 2021; Rios & Longoria, 2021), I argue that our commitment to helping novice teachers to thrive must honor and center the experiences and needs of BIPOC, disabled, LGBTQ+ and other educators living in the margins (Starr, 2018). In this vein, inspired by Universal Design for Learning, which encourages educators to provide multiple means of engagement, representation, and expression to optimize inclusive access for learners with disabilities (Center for Applied Special Technology [CAST], 2022), I like to remind my teacher candidates that "what's good for those placed in the margins is good for everyone." I believe this same concept can help us humanize dedicated early career teachers.

HUMANISTIC TEACHER DEVELOPMENT

In this book, I propose that examining teacher development through a critical lens of humanistic learning theory (Farmer, 2001) is a helpful framework for proactively supporting new teachers to flourish. As such, combining tenets from humanism and multicultural education (Alifah, 2018; Allen, 2000; Banks, 1993; Gay, 2010, 2014; Ladson-Billings, 1995; Paris & Alim, 2017), for new teachers to thrive, I characterize humanistic teacher development as the following:

- Honoring the fact that teachers are full human beings and thus attending to the "whole teacher" who is an emotional, intellectual, physical, mental, cultural, racialized, gendered, and spiritual person

- Facilitating opportunities for regular self-evaluation for new teachers to track their progress, set incremental goals, and embrace praxis
- Empowering new teachers to choose how they achieve their professional responsibilities by considering their identities, beliefs, values, strengths, goals, and school community context

Throughout this book, I will return to my view of humanistic teacher development as a lens. My goal is to offer you practical tools that honor teachers as complete, complex, and evolving human beings who are vital contributors to shaping our society.

HOW TO USE THIS BOOK

This book includes six thematic chapters and a conclusion. Chapter 1 provides you with a clear argument for why priming new teachers to thrive is not only necessary to bolster retention but will also improve K–12 student outcomes. This chapter concludes with my proposal for a new paradigm for supporting early career teachers so that they are equipped with the skills and attributes of thriving teachers. I then connect this paradigm to an overview of the rest of the book and the tools imparted.

Along with preservice and early career teachers, I invite teacher educators and early career mentors into this crucial conversation for two main reasons. First, scholars concerned with early career teacher retention suggest that teacher preparation programs could play an important role in proactively preparing candidates to thrive once they enter the profession (Shirazizadeh & Karimpour, 2019; Valtierra, 2016). Second, participants in strategic mentorship programs are shown to navigate the early learning curve more easily than new teachers without effective mentors (Headden, 2014; Sulis et al., 2022). Yet most teacher preparation programs have little time or resources to cultivate the tools needed for candidates to thrive once they cross the threshold from trainee to teacher. Furthermore, some school districts do not offer early career mentorship, and many that do are often underfunded, understaffed, and lack a consistent framework or policies and practices (Heubeck, 2021; Southern Regional Education Board [SREB], 2018). Thus, along with featuring topics that are important to new

Introduction

teachers, *Preparing Early Career Teachers to Thrive* provides teacher educators and mentors alike reliable and efficient tools to incorporate into their programming and conversations with preservice and new classroom teachers.

Given the range of readers who will benefit from this book, I designed it for flexible use. You could choose to read this book cover to cover or focus on chapters most relevant to your current concerns. Moreover, there are many ways to use the knowledge and resources I impart. For instance, teacher educators can integrate the content and strategies from each chapter into their coursework or workshops. In addition, early career mentors can infuse tools into teacher induction programs, one-on-one mentoring sessions, or professional learning communities (PLCs). Finally, new teachers can organize a book group to collectively work through the materials and empower one another to thrive. In each chapter that follows, I offer suggestions for how to infuse these tools into coursework, professional development workshops, one-on-one mentoring conversations, and book clubs.

While the problems of early career teacher burnout and attrition are immense, our collective commitment to proactively set up new teachers to thrive can instill a promising new trajectory where teachers flourish. Consequently, their students and schools can also thrive.

CHAPTER 1

Understanding Burnout to Turn It Around

Education is our passport to the future, for tomorrow belongs to the people who prepare for it today.

—Malcolm X

CHAPTER 1 GOALS

1. For readers to appreciate the direct relationship between teachers thriving and student achievement
2. For readers to understand the severity of national and global novice teacher turnover trends
3. For readers to understand causes of teacher burnout, disillusionment, and demoralization
4. For readers to understand the personal attributes and school conditions that support novice teachers to thrive

---

For over a quarter of a century, researchers have concluded that teacher quality is the most important school-related predictor of student achievement (Darling-Hammond, 2000; Hanushek et al., 1998; Lee, 2018; Maruli, 2014). For example, in 1998, Hanushek and colleagues analyzed 400,000 students in 3,000 schools and found that student achievement was directly related to teacher quality. In tandem, they discovered that school quality was the second most important determinant. Quality teachers who teach in effective schools equates to student achievement.

More recently, Lee (2018) found that students taught by a series of strong teachers had a statistically positive relationship with students' short-term academic growth and long-term educational success, including college completion. Findings from these studies and many others have pushed policymakers to advocate for high-quality teacher preparation and career-long professional development (Darling-Hammond, 2000; Ingersoll et al., 2019). Unfortunately, while these policies have helped alter teacher preparation programs and professional development at some level, we continue to have a teacher retention crisis that has detrimental effects on the educational experiences and outcomes of millions of youths.

Special education, mathematics, and science persistently experience the most significant teacher shortages. For example, a 2017–2018 U.S. Department of Education study reported that 47 states and the District of Columbia (DC) experienced shortages in math, 46 states and DC experienced special education teacher shortages, and 43 states experienced science teacher shortages (U.S. Department of Education Office of Postsecondary Education, 2017). Consequently, many schools have no choice but to rely on underqualified teachers to fill these positions. Unqualified teachers lack sufficient content knowledge and pedagogical skills to adequately support their students.

Early career teacher turnover is a crisis perpetuating chronic instability that directly affects students, schools, districts, and the entire public education landscape (Wronowski, 2020). Moreover, teacher churn is exceptionally costly. Studies estimate that it costs over $20,000 to replace each teacher who leaves an urban school district (Sutcher et al., 2016). Furthermore, reports indicate that some states spend up to $2.2 billion annually on teacher attrition (Alliance for Excellent Education [AEE], 2014). If schools had a more stable workforce, they could put their funding to better use, making teaching a more sustainable profession and improving student academic outcomes. Schools would have financial resources to reduce class sizes, invest in more teacher's aides, offer high-quality professional development and induction programs, purchase up-to-date technology, increase teacher salaries, and more. Each of these improvements would directly support student academic achievement.

Inadequate working conditions, an adverse school climate, ineffective school leadership, and top-down accountability pressures cause early career burnout and attrition (Wronowski, 2020). And, while the profession has grappled with teacher burnout and attrition for decades, the consequences are now more apparent than ever. COVID-19 exacerbated many educational inequities that existed pre-pandemic and caused additional teaching challenges. In 2020, teachers quickly shifted to remote teaching with little warning (Shedrow, 2021; Wu et al., 2020). In addition, most had to swiftly learn new formats (virtual, hybrid, in-person with COVID-19 protocols, etc.), which required mastering unfamiliar technologies (Baliram et al., 2021; Marshall et al., 2020), all while navigating the shared trauma of a global pandemic.

At present, the pressures of teaching since the COVID-19 pandemic have been immense. For example, a 2022 National Education Association (NEA) study reports that many previously thriving educators are now calling it quits. Furthermore, countless potential preservice teachers are changing their plans. Finally, survey results indicate that 90% of U.S. K–12 teachers feel burnout is a significant problem, and 55% plan to leave the profession sooner than initially planned (NEA, 2022). Along with the vast changes and pressures that COVID-19 has presented to the profession, for many teachers in the United States and other countries, the public education reform agenda has added to their dismay.

EDUCATION REFORM, TEACHER RECRUITMENT, AND RETENTION

Teachers are vital to shaping students, school systems, and societies. Young people spend the foundational decades of their lives in schools, and teachers play a major role in shaping the adults they become. Teachers can change the course of students' lives. Yet current education reform pressures are a significant source of teacher distress. Parker Palmer argued in *The Courage to Teach* (2017) that in our hurry to reform education: "We have forgotten a simple truth: reform will never be achieved by renewing appropriations, restricting schools, rewriting curricula, and revising texts if we continue to demean and dishearten the human resource called the teacher on whom so much depends . . . none of that will transform education if we fail to cherish—and challenge—the human heart that is the source of good teaching" (p. 4).

Many teachers do not feel cherished or respected by our education systems. They juggle multiple and often competing priorities that require them to answer to policymakers, administrators, colleagues, families, and more. And when teachers struggle to meet their job demands, their students ultimately suffer. Hence, we must rethink how we train and support novice teachers to equip them to give students their best. Teachers are crucial to students, school systems, and the future of societies. We should uplift them and ensure they are prepared for success.

Several studies have shown that between 40% and 50% of novice U.S. teachers exit the profession within the first 5 years of teaching (e.g., Kaden et al., 2016; Papay et al., 2015). This revolving door is most evident in under-resourced urban schools. For instance, a 2015 study of 16 urban districts by Papay and colleagues found an average 55% turnover rate for urban teachers in their first 5 years. Yet, while urban settings receive a lot of attention around the problem of teacher turnover, rural schools are also deeply impacted. For example, some studies report up to 50% of beginning rural teachers' turnover (Nguyen & Springer, 2021; Ulferts, 2016). In some locations, teacher turnover is higher in rural than urban school districts. For instance, in Arctic Alaska, many schools are in small high-poverty communities and experience excessive teacher attrition and low rates of retaining quality teachers (Kaden et al., 2016).

While the United Nations considers education a universal right (UNESCO, 2016a), we cannot deliver this human right without thriving teachers. The recruitment and retention of teachers is a global issue that most prominently affects under-resourced communities. Yet even Finland, a well-resourced country that holds teachers in high regard and has an innovative and highly accessible national education system, struggles with teacher retention. A 2020 large-scale Finnish longitudinal study found that 50% of surveyed teachers had turnover plans (Räsänen et al., 2020). Like teachers in several other countries including the United States, neoliberal educational reform pressures, including top-down decision-making, increased workload, and dwindling teacher autonomy, were the leading causes of Finnish turnover intentions (Ball, 2003; Lewis & Holloway, 2019; Räsänen et al., 2020; Weiner, 2020). Likewise, in her book *Supporting Teacher Wellbeing*, Suzanne Allies (2021) reports that loss of autonomy related to national education reform pressures in England is a significant cause of declining well-being and subsequent teacher turnover. High rates of burnout, feelings of disillusionment and demoralization steer many teachers, in a variety of contexts, to exit the profession prematurely.

TEACHER BURNOUT, DISILLUSIONMENT, AND DEMORALIZATION

Education scholars contend that burnout, disillusionment, and demoralization are common and interconnected phenomena contributing to teacher turnover (Molero-Jurado et al., 2019; Santoro, 2018; Valtierra, 2023).

Burnout

Burnout is characterized as a state of chronic stress that leads to:

- physical and emotional exhaustion,
- cynicism,
- detachment, and
- feelings of ineffectiveness and lack of accomplishment (Maslach & Leiter, 2016).

Burnout occurs when a teacher's initial passion for the work is extinguished. According to Nagoski and Nagoski (2019), 20% to 30% percent of U.S. teachers have moderately high to high levels of burnout. Moreover, they noted that, especially for women, emotional exhaustion adversely affects work, relationships, and physical health.

It is not hard to draw a parallel between the pressure teachers experience, their declining well-being, and symptoms of burnout. For example, when I was a 1st-year teacher working in an under-resourced urban school, I had a class of 32 3rd- and 4th-grade students. Most of my students lived at or below the poverty line, and many of their families struggled to meet their basic needs. Some of my students would come to school tired, undernourished, and some were navigating traumatic life circumstances. Their situation made it difficult for some to concentrate, and others struggled behaviorally. Moreover, I didn't have curriculum materials, books, or other necessary resources to meet their needs or interests. I spent my nights and weekends (and a heavy chunk of my paychecks) designing curriculum. I was deeply passionate about my beloved students and teaching them, but the stress and lack of rest and support eventually resulted in emotional and physical exhaustion (Valtierra, 2016). By the end of my first semester, I was on the road toward burnout.

I was not alone in my experience. In fact, Molero-Jurado and colleagues (2019) estimate that in the last 20 years, nearly 30% of teachers globally have reported experiencing burnout. Burnout decreases professional satisfaction, reduces commitment levels, and undermines health. Teacher burnout can lead many new educators to abandon the profession prematurely.

Disillusionment

Novice teachers are especially susceptible to burnout for several reasons. One main culprit is the intense early career learning curve. Consequently, it is common for new teachers to also experience a period of disillusionment. Teacher disillusionment occurs when a novice becomes disappointed as they discover that teaching is different than what they envisioned. For instance, in a 3-year study where I followed 10 early career urban teachers, I found that each participant experienced a period of what I named "structural disillusionment" because their primary source of disappointment was the ways that the system of education wasn't set up for their success (Valtierra, 2023).

My study found that novice teacher disillusionment had two main culprits. Foremost, there was a clear parallel between how systemic inequities of student poverty and trauma directly affected teachers' classrooms. My participants were determined to figure out how to create inclusive and trauma-informed classrooms, but they lacked time, training, resources, and administrative support. Second, top-down performative pressures, coupled with inadequate professional development to implement new practices, caused participants to feel disillusioned with their schools and the teaching profession.

Demoralization

Demoralization is another tension that many teachers experience. Educator demoralization is the "inability to access the moral rewards offered and expected in teaching" (Santoro, 2018, p. 8). For instance, common moral rewards associated with teaching include making a positive impact on students, learning with and from students, and helping students discover their passions. Doris Santoro studied 23 teachers with between 5 and 35 years in the classroom. Each of her participants had moral concerns about their work but remained in the profession during her study. Unlike the disillusionment experienced by new teachers (Moir, 1990), demoralization happens when teachers *can no longer* teach in a manner that aligns with their moral and ethical commitments to the profession. In other words, teachers experience demoralization when their personal beliefs are no longer aligned with their professional actions. Changes in school climate and administrator leadership style, prioritizing conformity to neoliberal policies and demands, lead to demoralization.

Santoro (2018) argues that demoralization is a phenomenon unique to experienced teachers. However, without robust support for novice teachers, those who survive the early years are still at risk for attrition. It seems plausible that as early career teachers become more experienced, and their initial disillusionment fades, they are still susceptible to demoralization.

Burnout, disillusionment, and demoralization can coexist, overlapping and therefore increasing teachers' likelihood of leaving the profession. These concerns are important because ultimately students are negatively affected when teachers experience high burnout, disillusionment, and/or demoralization. While these challenges are daunting, a dynamic interplay between personal attributes and contextual factors can help new teachers flourish so they stay in the profession and thrive (Jennings, 2020).

PERSONAL ATTRIBUTES OF THRIVING TEACHERS

The problems that lead to teacher recruitment and attrition are immense. Yet this book is focused on solutions, which require reframing how we train and mentor novice teachers. Having offered an overview of the complex problems that contribute to early career attrition, I now focus on reliable tools to prime early career teachers to thrive.

To begin with, education research studies suggest that personal attributes of identity, resilience, and agency operate interchangeably to contribute to a teacher's ability to thrive (Cobb, 2021; Day, 2018). Teacher identity is a continuing process of "interpretation and reinterpretation of who one considers oneself to be and who one would like to become" (van Lankveld et al., 2017, p. 326). A strong teacher identity can support one's capacity to teach according to their values and beliefs (Palmer, 2017). Teacher resilience describes their capacity to bounce back from adversity (Ainsworth & Oldfield, 2019). Resilience enhances feelings of effectiveness for early career teachers (Hong et al., 2018). Teacher agency refers to their active contribution to shaping their work and its conditions (Biesta et al., 2015). For beginning teachers, agency often depends on their self-confidence (Sulis et al., 2022).

Identity

Scholars agree that teacher identity is a fluid and complex construct that is difficult to define (Nichols et al., 2016; Schutz et al., 2019;

Truscott & Barker, 2020). Johnson and colleagues (2014) wrote that teacher identity development is the process of becoming aware of and making sense of oneself as a teacher. Novice teachers develop their identity by discovering what makes them unique, their beliefs and values around education, and how they will teach according to those beliefs and values. Teacher identity is in a continuous state of evolution. It requires the negotiation and renegotiation of a teacher's self as they simultaneously make sense of internal factors such as their emotions, dispositions, and self-efficacy and external factors inclusive of policy, school climate, teaching assignment, and professional development (Alsup, 2019; Schutz et al., 2019; Ticknor, 2014). The process of teacher identity formation is multifaceted and includes merging "agency, resilience, efficacy, attributions, and the need for vulnerability" (Schutz et al., 2019, p. 4). Teachers cannot separate professional and personal identities (Palmer, 2017). As a result, too little attention to the personal dimension of identity development contributes to novice teachers leaving the profession (Schaefer & Clandinin, 2018).

Despite the grim realities of teacher burnout and attrition, some teachers maintain their commitment to the profession and successfully navigate the tensions between their "call to teach" (Palmer, 2017) and the competing demands they juggle that can include adherence to standardization, testing, scripted curriculum, and other associated performative pressures. These demands do not typically align with a teacher's calling or emerging professional identity. In contrast, prominent multicultural education scholar Sonia Nieto (2005, 2013) inquired into the lives of effective teachers of diverse students and concluded that bringing their identities into the classroom was critical. Likewise, scholar and activist Parker J. Palmer argued that effective teaching requires "self-knowledge," and, therefore, attention to their "inner landscape" (2017, p. 3) is a central concern as educators navigate the current standardized reform climate. Moreover, my in-depth narrative study of a thriving 40-year veteran urban teacher found that her identity, including her beliefs, values, and optimistic attitude, was essential to her career longevity (Valtierra, 2016).

Resilience

Resilience is defined as a person's ability to bounce back from adversity. Research indicates that resilient teachers tend to feel more successful and stay in their positions longer than those who lack resilience

(Austin & Koerner, 2016; Huisman et al., 2010). While some scholars conceptualize resilience as an innate attribute (Gu & Day, 2007), others argue that teachers can acquire these qualities through supportive relationships, hopeful dispositions, self-reflection, and learning from mistakes (Castro et al., 2010; Howard & Johnson, 2004). Resilience enhances feelings of effectiveness for early career teachers (Hong et al., 2018). Moreover, the literature suggests that a growth mindset, self-care, centering students, and maintaining a hopeful disposition can contribute to early career teacher resiliency (Munroe, 2022; Tait, 2008).

Early career teaching is demanding and can contribute to psychological distress. New teachers often feel strained by the many expectations and scope of teaching; inconsistencies between their teacher training and the expectations of their new job; feelings of isolation and lack of support; and disillusionment (Tait, 2008). Teacher resilience can help novices manage and cope with these early career realities. Tait (2008) identified several trends in the capacities of novice teachers who demonstrated high degrees of resilience:

- Being self-starters who took advantage of opportunities to develop their skills in the classroom and adopt problem-solving strategies
- Rebounding and learning from difficult experiences
- Committing to self-care
- Maintaining an optimistic attitude

Furthermore, Munroe (2022) compared the resilience of a novice and a veteran music teacher who served in a high-poverty school committed to trauma-sensitive practices. Munroe found that the novice teacher was beginning to develop resiliency through two main strategies: attempting to understand students' lived experiences and maintaining a positive attitude.

Agency

Teachers experience agency when they have a degree of professional autonomy over their work and are active contributors to their teams. For beginning teachers, agency is often tied to their self-confidence (Sulis et al., 2022). School-level change usually requires teacher agency. Change is an inevitable aspect of the teaching profession. Teachers are responsible for implementing curricular and instructional changes as education research progresses and policies evolve. Teacher agency affects if and how they positively navigate change that supports student learning and a teacher's ability to thrive.

Pantić and colleagues (2022) studied teachers' understanding of change specific to improving inclusive classroom practices. Their analysis of two schools over 6 months suggested that teachers' daily professional activities of supporting students, lesson planning, and contributing to improved working conditions increased their agency for changing their practices to ensure inclusion. In other words, as these teachers began to implement inclusive practices through rethinking planning, student support, and advocating for improved working conditions, their agency increased. Their early agency led to more agency. In addition, this study suggested that novice teachers were more likely to exhibit agency for inclusive practices when they prioritized students' well-being and learning. Finally, Pantić and colleagues discovered that the teachers who acted as change agents developed diverse and collaborative professional networks.

Teacher identity, resilience, and agency are dynamically interconnected. For example, when a teacher is rooted in their identity, they are more likely to bounce back from the inevitable challenges that come with learning this new role because they can recalibrate their focus on their values. As they gain more experience and confidence, they are more apt to exercise their agency to align their identity with their practices. In this way, identity, resilience, and agency fundamentally reinforce each other (Day, 2018). This active interplay was evident in Cobb's (2022) in-depth study of four individual teachers during their first year. Cobb found that the 1st-year teachers' identities, resilience, and agency collectively helped them anticipate beyond challenges, pressure, and wavering confidence. Moreover, Trevethan (2018) found that early career teachers' reflection and self-awareness (promoting teacher identity development); personal resources, including self-regulation skills (which encourages resilience); and boundary setting (an agentive behavior) contributed to positive teaching experiences.

CONDITIONS FOR TEACHERS TO THRIVE

In tandem with personal attributes, several conditional factors are known to contribute to a teacher's ability to thrive, including targeted mentorship, an affirming school environment, administrator support, and strong collegial relationships (Allies, 2021; Hong et al., 2018; Sulis et al., 2022; Trevethan, 2018). Perrone and colleagues (2019) found that while some early career burnout is typical, school climate and how school administrators navigate accountability pressures directly affect the severity of novice burnout and subsequent turnover. Other researchers contend that administrators who promote a shared mission, set high standards, value teachers' self-interests, uphold teaching as meaningful work, and foster a positive environment create the conditions for teachers to thrive (Allies, 2021; Johnson, 2019).

Thoughtful and structured mentorship programs can help novices thrive. Zaharis (2019) found that novice teachers ranked mentorship from veteran teachers as highly important in supporting their practices and reducing feelings of stress. Similarly, Trevethan (2018) found that collaborative relationships with colleagues significantly contributed to beginning teachers' success. Moreover, Susan Moore Johnson's (2019) influential book *Where Teachers Thrive* explored 14 high-poverty urban schools to uncover conditions supporting teachers' professional growth and effectiveness. Johnson's findings highlight the vital role of school leaders in facilitating robust teacher hiring practices, collaborative planning and assessment, and professional development. The systems adopted by successful school leaders in Johnson's study supported teachers in thriving via comprehensive, mutually reinforcing strategies that fostered collaborative efforts for schoolwide improvement.

School leaders play an essential role in establishing the conditions for teachers to flourish. Moreover, administrators can directly contribute to teacher resilience and agency. For instance, two decades of research have found that developing positive relationships with colleagues who understand the realities of teaching, who reinforce the value of their work, and who offer insight and support as they learn to navigate a variety of teaching situations enhances novice teacher resilience (Tait, 2008). Hence, administrators should ensure novice teachers have positive mentors who can help them navigate the early career learning curve.

While teacher agency is considered a personal attribute, a novice's sense of agency is often encouraged or discouraged by administration, colleagues, and/or their school context.

As such, mentors and administrators can build early career teacher agency by cultivating collective trust, valuing their voices and pedagogical choices, and creating opportunities for them to implement their ideas (Reichenberg, 2022). Yakavets and colleagues (2022) discovered that novice teacher agency in education reform implementation increased when teachers believed in and had opportunities to dialogue about and develop professionally around the initiatives they needed to implement. In summary, novice teachers are more likely to build resiliency and agency when they have strong mentors and collegial relationships, and they are supported through professional development to understand and enact change.

A NEW PARADIGM FOR PREPARING AND SUPPORTING EARLY CAREER TEACHERS

Most teacher preparation programs emphasize the technical aspects of the profession—lesson planning and delivery, assessment, and methods for teaching 21st-century literacy and mathematical skills (Council for the Accreditation of Educator Preparation [CAEP], 2022; Ro, 2019). Later, when teachers transition into early career educators, professional development typically centers on refining their technical skills to improve student academic outcomes (McChesney & Aldridge, 2019). While technical skills are vital, they are futile if teachers burn out, become cynical, and quit before they have had enough time to develop their teaching craft. The literature suggests direct ways that school leaders and mentors can promote novice teacher resiliency and agency. Furthermore, scholars who study the professional identities of preservice and early career teachers have concluded that teacher preparation programs should prioritize candidates' identity development (Beijaard, 2019; Schaefer & Clandinin, 2018; Ticknor, 2014).

Hence, preservice and early career teachers need opportunities to build strong professional identities, resilience, and agency that can lead to their success. As depicted in Figure 1.1, the following chapters provide teacher educators, early career mentors, administrators, and novice teachers with specific tools to cultivate the personal attributes that can help them thrive. Moreover, I weave the development of these attributes into strategies that readers can use to create the conditions for novice teacher success.

Figure 1.1. Preparing Early Career Teachers to Thrive: Promoting Identity, Resilience, and Agency

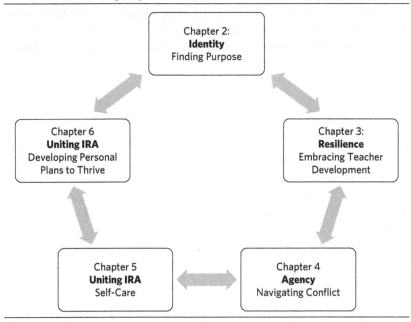

CONCLUSION: TEACHING TO THRIVE

The purpose of this chapter was to lay the groundwork for why investment in novice teacher development is crucial to education reform. The chapters that follow share firsthand anecdotes, insights, and strategies that I have collected over the last decade to prime preservice and early career teachers to flourish. In the following chapter, I will share how finding a clear purpose for teaching can support novice teacher identity development.

Teaching is heart-based work. People choose this work because they are enthusiastic about their discipline and passionate about youth. They want to make a difference. And yet learning to teach is hard work. Indeed, learning to implement curriculum while navigating classroom and school dynamics in their first few years of teaching is a lot of pressure. It's normal for novices to experience some burnout and disillusionment as they learn the ropes. I have yet to meet a 1st-year teacher who doesn't feel exhausted and a bit surprised by all that goes into their new role. However, there are ways to help mitigate their stress by proactively attending to their identity development, resiliency, and agency. This book will offer readers practical tools to both foster these personal attributes and cultivate the school conditions that encourage them. Throughout the book I will provide specific ways for teacher educators, early career mentors, and novice teachers to adopt the strategies I share.

CHAPTER 2

Sustaining Purpose
Creating an Authentic Teacher Identity

Good teaching cannot be reduced to technique; good teaching comes from the identity and integrity of the teacher.

—Parker Palmer, *The Courage to Teach*

CHAPTER 2 GOALS

1. For readers to understand what motivates people to choose teaching as a profession
2. To provide readers with tools designed to help preservice and early career teachers discover their purpose and begin to form their professional identity
3. To provide readers with assignments that help preservice and early career teachers to align their practices to their purpose
4. To share encouraging insights from preservice through 3rd-year teachers who participated in the exercises I detail

---

JAMES UPHOLDS HIS PURPOSE UNDER PRESSURE

During his teacher training, James viewed teaching as "a really meaningful, powerful way to do something in society and affect young people's lives and do something good in a system that isn't always so good." Like many of his high school students, James survived a traumatic upbringing. He hoped to "effect systemic change through being a positive role model" for his English students. To do this, James believed that "forming true relationships" with students and making the English curriculum "relatable to their background and goals" was the best way to effect change and be a positive role model (Research Interviews, 2019, 2020, 2021).

James was excited for his first teaching position at the urban high school where he previously student taught. He felt supported by his team and had already built strong relationships with the students. Despite these positive points, his under-resourced high school was "on watch" by the state for low performance, which made his first few years an emotional roller coaster. James and his colleagues faced pressure to raise test scores so the school would stay open. This urgency came with disjointed professional development and top-down pressures to swiftly adopt scripted curricula and uniform practices. James and his team felt their students were unmotivated by the curricular changes and noticed a decrease in attendance. While they were invested in school improvement, James and his peers felt that more strategic professional development, improved administrative systems, more resources, and trauma-sensitive practices were more appropriate pathways to school improvement. James and his team had to choose between conforming to standardized curricula or adapting materials to be relevant and meaningful to their diverse student body.

Although it wasn't easy, James did his best to maintain his identity as a "relatable and relevant teacher and role model" despite pushback from "higher-ups" who expected all classes to be "identical." By his third year, students in James's classes were making steady academic progress, and attendance rates were up. James reflected on his original purpose,

> I think it was a little bit naïve to think I could "change a system," but I am a good role model, I cheer the kids on and adapt to what kids care about and need . . . and as far as teaching goes, I'm not going to do anything else with my life. This is it.

What follows are insights and practices that helped James and other novice teachers sustain purpose and develop their identities as inspiring early career teachers!

*   *   *

Like James, most people choose to become a teacher for noble reasons. Over the years, people have often told me that they were inspired by the teachers who shaped them, or they wanted to be a role model and to contribute to positive social change. However, these aspirations are soon tested as early career teachers learn to navigate the tensions between their visions and the profession's stark realities. Many new teachers become disillusioned and unmotivated when they first experience the standardization and performativity that come with the job. Hence, one of my priorities in priming teachers to thrive is to help them discover their ultimate "why" for committing to this important work. The ultimate why, I've found, is the first step toward cultivating a meaningful teacher identity. When we establish and then prioritize our purpose for teaching, we are more likely to sustain our motivation to teach. In fact, the research is clear that most budding teachers have strong intrinsic and altruistic motivations to teach. Yet the standardization and performativity pressures of the profession are strong extrinsic forces that can easily distract and derail teachers from the deeper meaning of this work. When distracted or derailed from their purpose, teachers committed to equity can soon lose hope and agency to implement CSP. As such, I want new and aspiring teachers to have strategies to stay grounded in their ultimate "why" while simultaneously learning to balance the more technical and contingent aspects of their job.

This chapter offers a brief overview of what often motivates people to teach. I discuss the importance of making these motivations explicit to support novice teachers in their professional identity formation. Next, I detail assignment examples, reflective exercises, and strategies designed to support novice teachers in recognizing and staying grounded in their purpose. Finally, I share insights from teachers who used the tools I describe.

WHAT MOTIVATES US TO TEACH?

Career choice is frequently studied through the psychological construct of motivation (Fray & Gore, 2018). Psychologists define motivation as the process that inspires, guides, and maintains goal-oriented behaviors (Locke & Latham, 2002). Inspiration to become a teacher is frequently informed by a continuum of motivations ranging from seeing it as a practical professional choice to viewing our work as a calling. Concurrently, while most of the published research on why people teach is conceptualized from an empirical psychological framework, several educational philosophers look at teaching through a "spiritual" lens (Dantley, 2003; Lantieri, 2001; Noddings, 2005; Palmer, 2017), viewing it is a sacred act that contributes deeply to one's life purpose. Scholars of spirituality in education value the intersections between psychological motivations and the acute personal meaning, connectedness, and purpose that inspire many teachers (Dantley, 2003; Lantieri, 2001).

Psychological Motivations

Psychological research focuses on three types of motivation that influence a teacher's career choice: extrinsic, intrinsic, and altruistic motivation (Alvariñas-Villaverde et al., 2022; Dos Santos, 2020; Fray & Gore, 2018; Glutsch & König, 2019; Hennessy & Lynch, 2016; Htang, 2019; Lohbeck & Frenzel, 2021; Tamir, 2013). Choosing and sustaining a career in teaching is often a mix, to varying degrees, of these three forms of psychological motivation (Watt & Richardson, 2007, 2012).

Extrinsic motivation encapsulates the external rewards that teaching can offer (Fray & Gore, 2018; Htang, 2019; Lohbeck & Frenzel, 2021). Some educators are extrinsically motivated to pursue teaching for a balanced lifestyle that summers off and flexible working hours can offer. Others are inspired by conditions such as job security, a positive working environment, a reliable income, and/or opportunities for career advancement. For instance, for myself, as a working parent, having summers and holidays off to spend with my family is an extrinsic motivator for teaching.

Intrinsic motivations encompass personally rewarding factors to teachers (Alvariñas-Villaverde et al., 2022; Glutsch & König, 2019; Hennessy & Lynch, 2016; Lohbeck & Frenzel, 2021; Mobra & Hamlin, 2020). The scholarship most frequently notes that teachers are intrinsically motivated by their passion for the act of teaching and/or a particular subject, interest in and finding joy in teaching and being with youth, feeling suited for the work, feelings of accomplishment, and/or, the intellectual stimulation and personal development that come with teaching. For example, one of my intrinsic motivators is the fact that as a teacher I am always learning and discovering. In other words, it's hard to get bored with teaching!

Altruistic motivations center around the well-being of others and society at large (Alvariñas-Villaverde et al., 2022; Dos Santos, 2020; Htang, 2019; Mobra & Hamlin, 2020; Tamir, 2013). Studies have found that altruistic motivations influence a teacher's desire to be of service to others, help and support students, make a difference, contribute to society, and/or answer a calling. Personally, I feel called to teach. From an altruistic motivation standpoint, teaching is my purpose and simultaneously allows me to contribute to society in productive ways.

Studies have shown that aspiring teachers are most motivated by intrinsic and altruistic values. Moreover, research indicates that preservice teachers are least motivated for extrinsic reasons (Fray & Gore, 2018). Hence, while extrinsic motivations are indeed a part of

Sustaining Purpose   31

why people choose to teach, focusing on intrinsic and altruistic motivations may help foster teachers' identities and sustain their commitment to the profession.

Deep Purpose and Teacher Identity

It is not hard to draw a parallel between the empirical psychological conceptions of intrinsic and altruistic motivations for teaching and the ideas of spirituality-in-education scholars. Theorists characterize teacher spirituality as related to personal meaning, connectedness, and purpose (Dantley, 2003; Lantieri, 2001). One parallel to psychological motivation scholarship is how intrinsic motivation entails feeling *personally rewarded* by teaching and finding joy in *connecting with students*. A second parallel is connected to altruistic motivations, since these are *purpose driven*. Teachers are often altruistically motivated by giving back and contributing to society at large. In this way, the deeper meaning or spirit of teaching is another way of thinking about teacher motivation—and can contribute to understanding teacher motivation and identity formation (Noddings, 2005; Palmer, 2017; Valtierra & Michalec, 2017).

Parker J. Palmer is one of the most prominent scholars of teacher spirituality. In his popular book *The Courage to Teach*, he wrote that "teaching holds a mirror to the soul. If I am willing to look in that mirror and not run from what I see, I have a chance to gain self-knowledge—and knowing myself is as crucial to good teaching as knowing my students and my subject" (2017, p. 3). For over 20 years, Palmer has noted thriving teachers have a "strong sense of personal identity that infuses their work" (p. 11). Like identity scholars who argue that teacher identity development is deeply rooted in personal identity (Schaefer & Clandinin, 2018; Schutz et al., 2019; Ticknor, 2014), Palmer views teacher identity as sitting in "the diverse forces that make up" a teacher's life. He ties teacher identity to integrity, which "lies in relating those forces in ways that bring wholeness and life rather than fragmentation and death" (p. 14). Fragmentation and death, according to Palmer, are perpetuated by the fear-based practices of neoliberal reform mandates—including the standardization and performance pressures teachers juggle—which are often in opposition to the motivations of many new educators. Finally, Palmer argues that "good teaching cannot be reduced to technique; good teaching comes from the identity and integrity of the teacher" (2017, p. 10). A teacher's identity is tightly linked to their motivations for teaching. When a teacher has an inspiring purpose for the work, they can formulate an identity that connects to that purpose.

Inspired by Palmer's work and other scholars of spirituality in teaching (Dantley, 2003; Lantieri, 2001; Noddings, 2005), one of my priorities in priming teachers to thrive is to help them discover their ultimate "why" for committing to this important work. Discovering their ultimate why can help early career teachers maintain focus on their purpose and support a positive professional identity.

SUPPORTING NOVICE TEACHERS TO DISCOVER PURPOSE AND IDENTITY

There are several ways that I have supported novice teachers in discovering their purpose for choosing to teach and cultivate their teacher identity. Foremost, as an education department, my colleagues and I routinely ask our teacher candidates to name *why* they teach. This is a question they revisit throughout their programming. To start, when we interview program applicants, the first question we ask is "why teach?" Then, during program orientation, while candidates introduce themselves, one of our prompts is again "why teach?" This same question is asked at the beginning of each new course and any other chance we get. As a step toward grounding them in purpose, I find this is the essential question to keep at the front of their mind in their teacher preparation journey. By routinely acknowledging and often rethinking or revising their ultimate why, budding teachers are constantly reminded of their intrinsic and altruistic motivations.

Second, I facilitate a workshop session on the topic of purpose, and, taking cues from Parker Palmer (2017), I tie the concept of purpose to his notion of teacher identity and integrity. I then circle back to this throughout the rest of our programming. Finally, I've found it fruitful to infuse purpose-oriented assignments into my teaching methods coursework. These assignments are deliberately designed for novice teachers to learn how to embed their purpose and teacher identity into their classroom practices. What follows is an overview of the workshop session and a description of a "Theory to Practice Project" I use in my inclusive teaching methods course.

Naming Present Purpose Exercise

As they discover the purpose, early career teachers I work with often find the introduction and Chapter 1 of Palmer's (2017) *The Courage*

Sustaining Purpose   33

to Teach inspiring to read. The introductory chapter offers the reader an inspiring overview of teaching as "heart-based" or spiritually motivated work. Chapter 1 unpacks Palmer's belief that good teachers have a "strong sense of personal identity that infuses their work" (p. 11). Furthermore, through storytelling of personal and observed cases, Palmer illustrates the interconnectedness of teacher identity and integrity. My early career teacher participants are often motivated to discuss this poignant reading, which can serve as inspiration in discovering their "ultimate why."

I ask each participant to name their current why for teaching and the most important insight they took away from the Palmer readings. I then read and display the following quote from Palmer's introduction and invite the group to dialogue and collectively make sense of it:

"Technique is what teachers use until the real teacher arrives" (p. 6).

This often leads to a lively conversation about the tensions surrounding learning the technical aspects of teaching and navigating standardized curriculum while simultaneously developing a genuine teacher identity.

Reflection on Purpose Prompts

I often invite early career teacher participants to independently write in their reflection journal about the above quote and the following related question posed by Palmer (2017): *"Who is the self that teaches?"* (p. 4).

To break down this philosophical question for participants, I also include the following related questions:

- What parts of your identity can be leveraged to connect with your students?
- How will you bring your authentic self into your teaching?
- How does being a teacher influence your overall identity both inside and outside of your professional life?

I emphasize that Palmer's question is dynamic and iterative—meaning the question is never fully answered and responses will continuously transform as teachers evolve.

Figure 2.1. Drawing Wisdom From Inspiring Teachers: Reflection Prompts

1. Think back to the best, most inspiring teacher you have experienced in your education. In your reflection journal, list words or phrases and/or record images that describe the following:
   - What did they do?
   - What did they say?
   - How did they make you feel?
2. Turn and talk with a peer. For each partner's chosen teacher, collectively ponder the following:
   - Given that Palmer notes that "we teach who we are," who is this teacher?
   - What motivates them to teach? What is their purpose as a teacher?
   - What is the relationship between this teacher's purpose and their identity?
   - What do these inspiring teachers have in common?
   - What can you learn from these teachers as you work to solidify your purpose and form your teacher identity?

Unearthing Wisdom Exercise

I've also found the exercise depicted in Figure 2.1 fruitful. We typically debrief the exercise and look for common themes between the various inspiring teachers.

Envisioning the Future to Sustain Purpose Exercise

While for most teacher candidates retirement is a long way into the future, I've found that the exercise that follows in Figure 2.2 helps them remember that actualizing their purpose is an evolutionary process.

After we dialogue and share insights from Figure 2.2, I ask participants to ruminate on Palmer's question *"Who is the self that teaches?"* (p. 4) and note if and how they have gained clarity on this dynamic question.

Figure 2.2. Envisioning the Future Reflection Prompts: Your Retirement Party

Travel far into the future to your retirement party! You've had a thriving career as an inspiring teacher. Draft the keynote speech that will be delivered at the party by a beloved former student. Keep the following in mind:

1. What did you stand for as a teacher?
2. What legacy are you leaving behind?
3. What do former students, colleagues, and community members remember you for?

INFUSING PURPOSE AND PRACTICE IN PEDAGOGY

Translating our purpose to our practices—in other words, translating theory into practice—is a learning curve. As such, I emphasize praxis in all my teacher preparation coursework. According to educational philosopher Paulo Freire (1970), praxis is conceptualized as "reflection and action upon the world in order to transform it" (p. 52). Teachers can enact an ongoing cycle of praxis via reflecting, acting on those reflections, reflecting on the action, and revising actions based on their reflections. For example, a teacher can reflect on how they want to introduce a lesson to students, then introduce the lesson, reflect on how it went, and adapt their practices for next time based on those reflections. To help teacher candidates translate the theories they are learning about, and the theories they are developing about their teacher identities, into tangible actions in their classrooms, I try to design deliberate assignments that encourage praxis. One of the most popular assignments from my inclusive teaching methods course is the Theory to Practice Project. As shown in Figure 2.3, my syllabus explains:

Figure 2.3. Theory to Practice Project

This assignment is an opportunity to demonstrate your ability to merge your philosophy of education and emerging teacher identity with inclusive instructional practices. You will complete the following steps:

1. **Umbrella Goals:** Umbrella goals answer the question: *If students only took one semester of your class (or you teach them for only one semester at the elementary level), what would you want them to come away with?* These goals are based on course readings, discussion, your content standards, as well as your why and evolving philosophy of education. Limit your goals to 12 overarching essential ones. These goals are broad enough to cover any age level, thus are not detailed content objectives. Umbrella goals are developed and submitted two times, at the beginning and end of the course. Revised goals must show careful attention to instructor feedback and insights gained throughout the course.
2. **Personalized Planning Template:** Your customized lesson-planning template can be adapted from published sources or provided templates, and should be general enough that it can be filled in for any lesson you teach. It will need to include areas that you want to remember to address and a structure that supports your teaching and student learning, and applies course learning objectives. Furthermore, your template will reflect and demonstrate how you will put your umbrella goals into practice. You will have opportunities to plan and revise your template as you use it for lesson planning.

Teacher candidates provide a list of their umbrella goals for the first iteration. Then toward the end of the course, once they have had plenty of exposure and practice with inclusive teaching methods—which allows them to see how to translate coursework into classroom practices—the second version asks them to name exactly *how* they will reach those goals. Figure 2.4 is an example of Summer's final umbrella goals. Summer is now a thriving kindergarten teacher!

Then, throughout the inclusive teaching methods course, teacher candidates plan and teach from a variety of lesson formats. While one of my goals is for candidates to learn specific teaching methods, my final goal is for them to link method to their purpose, as I will illustrate below. To begin, some of our favorite lesson formats for practicing methods include:

- Harry and Sally Wong's (Wong & Wong, 2018) Teach, Rehearse, and Reinforce (T-R-R) method from *The Classroom Management Book*. Focused on establishing effective classroom routines, Wong and Wong's format guides teachers to model a specific classroom routine, rehearse the routine with students, and then reinforce the routine until it becomes an ingrained habit.
- Socorro Herrera's (2022) Activate, Connect, Affirm (A-C-A) from her book *Biography-Driven Culturally Responsive Teaching*. Focused on ensuring lesson plans are culturally responsive to the needs of CLD learners, this format guides teachers to begin a lesson by activating students' prior knowledge about the lesson content, connect new information to prior knowledge, and affirm students' new learning.
- Vacca et al.'s (2021) Before, During, and After (B-D-A) method for teaching reading in their textbook *Content Area Reading*. Focused on integration of content area reading, this template guides teachers to ensure they support meaning-making before, during, and after reading content area text.
- McTighe and Wiggins's (2005) *Understanding by Design* (UbD) curriculum development process. Commonly known as backward design, or beginning with the end in mind, this method guides curriculum development by guiding teachers to unpack standards and learning objectives, develop assessments that measure objectives, and then plan projects, assignments, and daily lessons accordingly.

Figure 2.4. Summer's Umbrella Goals

Why I teach: I teach because I feel most *alive* when I am with children! I teach ***to grow*** kind, curious, reflexive, and empowered young minds! Ultimately, I teach out of ***hope***.

Upon leaving my classroom, it is my hope that you will carry with you the abilities to . . .	Therefore, I must . . .
1. Make meaning of what kindness is and be a role model for what kindness looks like. You have the power to be a kindness ambassador everywhere you go.	Model kindness in all my interactions. We will work together to observe and practice kindness with the goal of becoming kindness ambassadors for our communities.
2. Internalize that your identity and background are an asset and unique gift. These gifts are a tool to help you learn, grow, and broaden the perspectives of others.	Create a classroom environment that displays and honors your identities, your interests, and your inquiries. We will work together to build a space that values who we are and that proudly displays our identities.
3. Embrace talking about ideas that are different from your own and learn to value these experiences because they will help you stay open-minded.	Model the ways in which we can be critical of what we think we know by always asking *why*. We will be inquirers and explorers of the varying narratives that we encounter through read-aloud, class discussions, and in the world around us.
4. Embody the spirit of play. Be unafraid to be a child, be creative, be curious, and be yourself.	Be patient and open to the nature of childhood. Sometimes work may get messy. Sometimes work may get noisy. And in the learning process, often, this creativity and collaboration is necessary.
5. Persevere even when you think something is too hard. It is the process, not the product, that will help you to learn.	Scaffold your learning to support your individual needs as a learner. I will challenge you to learn and grow, and I will be there to support you in the process. Your persistence will be rewarded through learning and discovery.
6. Value the process of reflection. When you think about where you have come from and where you are now, you give yourself choice in where you want to go.	Encourage you to talk and write about how you are feeling and what you are thinking. We will work together to set goals, achieve these goals, and to reflect on our goals to become self-reflective and self-directed learners.
7. Question. The human brain is special because it allows us to be curious. Use this curiosity because it is your superpower.	Permit and encourage questioning. We will work together to ask questions, search for answers, and use this search to lead us to more questions. Through questioning, we can unlock one of the greatest keys to learning—the search to know more.

Given their experiences with various lesson-planning methods, teacher candidates are often eager to consolidate what they have learned and merge their practical skills with their umbrella goals. Essentially, the second part of the Theory to Practice Project challenges candidates to merge their purpose, via umbrella goals, with their classroom practices through designing their own lesson plan template that is informed by the research. Figures 2.5 to 2.7 show Summer's personalized planning

Figure 2.5. Summer's Personalized Planning Template: Part 1

Lesson Logistics		
Title	Subject	Mindset: What frame of mind will I model and support my students to embody? *(UG #1)
Pacing	Phase 1: _____ minutes Phase 2: _____ minutes Phase 3: _____ minutes	
Materials		
Standards and Big Ideas		
Content Standards		Specific Skills
Common Core: State/District:		The skills my students will build through this lesson are:
Lesson Objectives in Student-Friendly Language		
Today we are. . . . . So that we can. . . . . We'll know we've got it when . . . *(UG #6)		
Essential Question(s)		Umbrella Goal(s)
Understandings		Related Misconceptions

Figure 2.6. Summer's Personalized Planning Template: Part 2

Disciplinary Literacy Considerations	
Key Vocabulary	Critical Literacy
What key vocabulary is essential to access this lesson? To add to our vocabulary bank?	How will I encourage my students to question "why"? What tools must my students be equipped with to question "why"? *(UG #3 & 7)

(continued)

Figure 2.6. (*continued*)

Culturally Sustaining Considerations	
Background Knowledge & Prior Context	
Who are we? Where have we been? Where do we need to end up? Why is this important? *(UG #2 & 6)	
Readiness	
How will I ensure this lesson is relevant to student lived experiences, cultural frameworks, interests, developmental stages? What content might I need to front-load to ensure that my students are ready for this lesson? *(UG #2)	
Universal Design for Learning	Differentiated Instruction
Engagement: Representation: Action and Expression: *(UG #2, 4 & 5)	For Content: For Process: For Product: *(UG #2, 4 & 5)

Figure 2.7. Summer's Personalized Planning Template: Part 3

Lesson Plan Outline
Before (reading lessons)/**Activation** (content lessons)/**Teach** (procedural lessons)
Hook Activity: **During** (reading lessons)/**Connection** (content lessons)/**Rehearse** (procedural lessons) Opportunities for collaboration: Connections with other content and prior knowledge: *(UG # 4)
After (reading lessons)/**Affirmation** (content lessons)/**Reinforce** (procedural lessons)
Synthesis and opportunities for transfer: Opportunities for student reflection & self-assessment: *(UG # 6)
Assessment
How will I assess my students to know if they have achieved learner outcomes? How will I provide specific, timely, meaningful, and goal-oriented feedback? *(UG # 7)
Backup Plan
Time Savers: What is my plan if we run out of time? **Extensions:** How might I extend for student transfer of knowledge, skills, &/ or understandings?

(*continued*)

Figure 2.7. (*continued*)

Praxis
How did my students respond to this lesson? Did the lesson go as I expected it to? Why or why not? How can I improve this lesson for next time? Did this lesson embody my teacher identity and integrity to my umbrella goals? Why or why not?

template, broken into three parts for readability purposes, with areas noted with * to signal how she merged theory to practice via connecting her umbrella goals to her template.

Over the years, many of our alumni comment that the Theory to Practice Project was highly impactful in helping them to discover their unique approach to planning and teaching. In fact, many continue to use and adapt their umbrella goals and personalized template in their professional career.

Figure 2.8. Chapter 2 Suggestions on How to Incorporate These Tools

Teacher Educators:
- Find every chance you get for teacher candidates to articulate *why* they want to be a teacher. Establish a routine wherein every new course, meeting, mixer, etc. includes members sharing their current "why." Explicitly share your "why"!
- Incorporate these tools into relevant coursework and/or workshops.
- Include a program-long written or audio reflection journal, personal blog, or website with purpose and teacher identity prompts I share.
- Be deliberate about connecting the technical aspects of teaching (standards, lesson plans, policies, etc.) to purpose and teacher identity formation.

Mentors:
- Begin meetings with mentees articulating why they teach. This will help new teachers keep their purpose front and center.
- Incorporate this workshop and Theory to Practice Project into your teacher induction professional development sessions. This could be presented live, as virtual recorded materials, or in a hybrid fashion.
- Then make sure school administrators and other supervisors know about, understand the value of, and ask about teachers' purpose, umbrella goals, and planning templates.
- Finally, use novice teachers' purpose, umbrella goals, and personalized planning templates as a coaching tool. Refer to these documents when supporting planning, goal setting, and mentee self-assessment.

New Teachers:
- Read Palmer's *The Courage to Teach* as book club. Use the prompts and exercises I share to guide your discussions and related activities.

(continued)

Sustaining Purpose

Figure 2.8. (*continued*)

- Find a creative and inspiring way to display and remind yourself daily of your purpose. Early career teachers I know have created posters and other artistic representations of the ultimate why to display in their classroom.
- Develop and put your own umbrella goals and personalized planning template in a place where you can easily refer to it, such as on your phone or desktop. Have these close by to guide your planning and reflection.

INSIGHTS FROM PRESERVICE AND EARLY CAREER TEACHERS

Over the years, my analysis of early career teacher reflections and our conversations about the purpose-oriented exercises shared in this chapter have illuminated a few consistent and inspiring ideas. Foremost, like the scholarship on motivations to enter teaching described at the beginning of the chapter, my participants consistently named altruistic, intrinsic, and/or spiritual motivations to teach. Their most common reasons include seeing teaching as the following:

- Social justice and/or political change work
- A way to empower youth as social change agents
- A way to give back to their communities
- A work of passion and/or joy
- Creative, intellectual, and/or spiritually stimulating work
- A way to honor inspiring teachers from their past
- A calling

For instance, Niki shared that "I teach because kids inspire me to think in new ways, but also to hopefully help them discover their own talents and purpose and skills to thrive in society." Similarly, Sara reflected that:

> I teach because I enjoy it. I teach because I want to help create people who can think critically about systems and inequalities and hopefully go forward into the world and effect change. I'd like to keep empowering future generations to improve our world.

While teachers had a range of unique "ultimate why's" for teaching, there were two common themes that they continuously ruminated on during our time together. Foremost, their desire for authenticity was a common through-line. For the budding educators who have participated in the ultimate why activities I described, developing and sustaining an authentic teacher identity was significant. Like James, whom we met at the beginning of this chapter, these teachers wanted to stay true to their purpose and dedication to CSP, even when they faced obstacles. Second, participants identified engagement in praxis as vital to sustaining their purpose. They deeply valued the iterative process of critical reflection, action, and reflection on action, and many of them pointed out that the Theory to Practice Project helped them maintain their commitment to praxis by deliberately including it in their lesson-planning process.

Authentic Teacher Identities

Time and again, the early career teachers who have participated in the exercises I described in this chapter commonly named their desire for authenticity as vital to their emerging teacher identities and ability to thrive. For instance, Katherine wrote that to "stay true to your authentic self, you need frequent reminders of who you are" and mentioned the importance of "noting areas that feel forced and inauthentic." Novice teachers most frequently recognized that authenticity requires "vulnerability," "teaching from the heart," "teaching who you are," "teaching with integrity," and being "open and honest" with students. TTLC participants were committed to continuous self-knowledge and recognized their teacher identities were not separate from the "other parts of my selfhood" but instead are, as Delia put it "an extension of myself." To maintain authenticity, some participants articulated plans to do "what I feel and believe" and, as Jeffrey wrote, "doing what is right, rather than what is on the test." Finally, the theme of self-care as a tool to maintain identity was a common sentiment. These new educators recognized that being a teacher is part of their "identity" and "a lifestyle." As Lexie put it:

> I firmly believe that as a teacher, life and work are not two separate entities, like you are the same human in your life and your work. . . . I think inherently they should be intertwined, but I think that you do need to, as a teacher, take care of yourself.

Authenticity Through Praxis

To sustain their teacher identities, the early career teachers I have supported commonly identified a commitment to praxis, the ongoing

Sustaining Purpose

interdependent process of action and reflection on action (Freire, 1970) as vital. Praxis, participants wrote, requires "self-reflection," "self-understanding," and openness to "lifelong learning." Teachers commonly articulated a commitment to "continuous reflection," "checking in with myself," balancing "self-reflection and feedback," and becoming, as Jordan wrote, "reflective of my teaching and not afraid of experimenting." Casey noted that praxis requires a commitment to the "understanding of self and others." Moreover, participants wrote that continuous "learning and growth" will encourage persistent identity formation and, consequently, help maintain integrity to their purpose. Teachers shared a commitment to trying new teaching approaches to "see what works for me," enduring "goal setting," and being "comfortable being uncomfortable" to evolve and teach with integrity.

Early career teachers commonly spoke of committing to praxis to uphold their identities and ultimate why. In addition, they spoke of praxis as a tool to self-assess and maintain a hopeful attitude about their teaching and the education system. Participants viewed praxis as a routine to "see the progress I have made," "set new goals for myself," and "find the positive" and "hopeful" moments. These novice teachers emphasized staying grounded in their why for choosing to teach and focusing on the intangible benefits—or intrinsic and altruistic motivations—of teaching. As Liz put it, "one of the big rewards of teaching is that there is a kind of reward built into it that can't really be quantified."

From a practical standpoint, the Theory to Practice Project was consistently recognized as a favorite by my teacher candidates as it helped them "create a very concrete path to incorporating theory and praxis into my daily practice." As a 3rd-year teacher, Lexie recalled this project:

> I am still really proud of the template I produced and the direction it took me in my teaching. The project made me feel like I had tangible routes to actually get my students to attain my Umbrella Goals and for me to commit to daily reflection. That felt really rewarding.

CONCLUSION: TEACHER IDENTITY FORMATION

It is common for aspiring teachers to be motivated for altruistic, intrinsic, and/or spiritual reasons. In essence, these motivations speak to my conception of humanistic teacher development. The central tenets of humanistic teacher development include:

- Honoring the fact that teachers are full human beings and thus attending to the "whole teacher" who is an emotional, intellectual, physical, mental, cultural, racialized, gendered, and *spiritual* person;
- Facilitating opportunities for regular self-evaluation for new teachers to track their progress, set incremental goals, and *embrace praxis*, and;
- Empowering new teachers to choose how they achieve their professional responsibilities by considering their *identities, beliefs, values*, strengths, goals, and school community context.

Yet standardized and performative-based expectations can cause tensions among teachers' motivations, purpose, and identities. This friction can often lead new teachers to feel deflated and dehumanized. I have found that to counteract these pressures, the ultimate why exercises and assignment ideas I detailed in this chapter can support novice teachers in realizing their full potential, and hence their full humanity as promising educators!

CHAPTER 3

Teaching Is Developmental

Promoting Resilience to Traverse
the Learning Curve

Have patience with all things but first of all with yourself.

—Francis de Sales

CHAPTER 3 GOALS

1. For readers to understand early career teacher development
2. To provide readers with tools designed to encourage preservice and early career teachers to understand, embrace, and reflect on their developmental journey
3. To share encouraging insights from preservice through 3rd-year teachers who participated in the teacher development exercises I detail

---

LIZ'S JOURNEY TOWARD RESILIENCE

While her student teaching experience in a middle-class 5th-grade classroom with a master teacher was smooth sailing, Liz's 1st-year teaching in a neighboring urban school district was an incredibly bumpy road. Describing herself as "barely surviving," Liz benefited from her highly supportive colleagues and administration but struggled to manage her classroom. The reality shock came from her 4th-graders' wide range of needs, including a large number of refugee children who were just learning English and acclimating to a new culture, several students receiving special education services for academic and/or behavioral support, most students reading far below grade level, and many navigating poverty and trauma. By spring of her first year, Liz's idealistic visions of fostering a harmonious classroom community were thwarted. Instead, "just showing up every day and giving everyone in the classroom and myself a blank slate" was her daily motto (Research Interviews, 2019 & 2021).

Despite a rocky first year, each year got better. Liz stayed in her school, motivated by the staff and administration, who were "the best team anyone could wish for," and her "incredibly funny, quirky, and awesome kiddos." By her third year, Liz was thriving. At the close of that year, Liz felt she "couldn't imagine not being a teacher—it's who I am!" and recognized that being patient with herself, leaning on trusted colleagues, and "celebrating little triumphs" got her through the initial learning curve.

What follows are insights and reflection exercises that helped Liz and other novice teachers become resilient, thriving teachers as they traversed the early career learning curve!

*   *   *

Like Liz, all new teachers struggle to learn the ropes. Yet they often feel alone and need reassurance that learning to teach is a lifelong endeavor. Hence, this chapter provides readers with an overview of early career teacher development. I then detail strategies to support new teachers in understanding, reflecting on, and setting developmental goals. Finally, I share insights from preservice and early career teachers who engaged with the tools I describe in this chapter. Their reflections show how the tools helped them acknowledge that having patience can support them in thriving. If we can keep in mind that learning to teach is a process, we can appreciate moments of triumph and frame the hard parts as temporary learning opportunities on the journey to becoming a thriving teacher!

TEACHER DEVELOPMENT

Scholars often refer to teacher development as the "teacher career cycle" (Fessler & Christiansen, 1992) or "life cycle" (Steffy et al., 2000). This body of work concerns teachers' progression, growth, and stages, spanning from student teaching through retirement (Bressman et al., 2018). There are three broad stages of teacher development I will discuss: early career, middle career, and late career (Coutler & Lester, 2011; Eros, 2011; Hargreaves, 2005; Mitchell, 2008). General characteristics of teachers at each of these stages include:

- **Early career (approximately preservice–5 years):** Early career teachers often lack professional confidence and typically function in "survival mode" (Christensen & Fessler, 1992; Huberman, 1993). New teachers focus on their own professional needs with specific attention to classroom management, curriculum mastery, and content delivery (Coutler & Lester, 2011). In addition, early career teachers require mentorship and opportunities to set goals, reflect, and self-assess (Bressman et al., 2018).
- **Middle Career (approximately 5–15 years):** Thriving mid-career teachers are confident and comfortable with the curriculum and their pedagogy (Hargreaves, 2005; Huberman, 1993). Mid-career teachers have shifted from focusing on their own professional needs and can prioritize their students' needs. Teachers at this stage are often motivated to seek opportunities to enhance their pedagogical skills to improve student learning (Coutler & Lester, 2011; Eros, 2011).
- **Late career (typically 15 years–retirement):** Thriving veteran teachers have stable teacher identities (Bressman et al., 2018). These seasoned teachers seek opportunities to deepen their expertise, explore various teaching and learning approaches, and experience student learning as connected to community context and broader social issues (Coutler & Lester, 2011; Mitchell, 2008).

The Ebbs and Flows of Novice Teaching

To prime preservice and early career teachers to thrive, it is helpful to understand the ebbs and flows of transitioning from teacher in training to early career educator. Several teacher development scholars have closely examined this foundational period (e.g., Feiman-Nemser, 2001; Fessler & Christiansen, 1992; Huberman, 1993; Steffy et al., 2000). While most of these studies occurred 20–30 years ago, their frameworks continue to inform how we understand teacher development (e.g., Eros, 2011; Headden, 2014; Kelchtermans, 2017; Valtierra, 2022). However, while helpful in making sense of the early career life cycle, it is also essential to acknowledge that the following themes are general approximations. Each teacher will experience variability based on their personal and environmental context.

In the early 2000s, Betty Steffy and colleagues proposed the Life Cycle Model for Career Teachers. Informed by both the teacher development literature and systemic observation of teachers over time, the Life Cycle Model for Career Teachers is a developmental model that features a continuum of phases that denote excellence in teaching across the career span. Given that the early career phases of the Life Cycle Model bridge preservice and inservice teacher development, this continuum is a helpful lens to appreciate early career progression.

Teachers in Training. Since learning to teach is a developmental process, scholars contend that teacher preparation should lay the groundwork for priming aspiring educators as lifelong learners (Feiman-Nemser, 2001; Sunthonkanokpong & Murphy, 2019). In other words, it is important to remember that while teacher preparation is vital, it is only the beginning of a teacher's developmental journey. Teaching is a complex, dynamic, recursive, and acquired skill.

Typically, after completion of coursework, the final phase of traditional teacher preparation entails full-time student teaching. The goal of student teaching is for preservice teachers to take on the day-to-day work of a professional teacher under the guidance of an experienced cooperating teacher and a faculty member from their teacher preparation program. Essential to connecting coursework to practice, student teaching offers hands-on experience in the classroom. This is often the first-time aspiring teachers have their idealism tested as they discover that teaching is messy, nuanced, and continually responsive to "in the moment" occurrences (Giboney Wall, 2016).

According to the Life Cycle Model for Career Teachers, student teaching is the exploration phase of teacher development. Student teachers are beginning to acquire their professional identity and require opportunities to take risks and learn through trial and error. They often experience tensions between the "best practices" they studied in coursework and how teaching actually plays out in the classroom. It is also common for them to feel overwhelmed by the many tasks that teachers juggle. Finally, they often experience competing emotions including anxiety, frustration, disillusionment, joy, fear, and insecurity.

During this foundational phase, student teachers tend to focus on mastering lesson design and delivery. With their energy focused on the classroom, they are often naïve about the many organizational, administrative, and interpersonal factors that come with the job. For instance, reminiscing about his student teaching experience, 1st-year teacher James expressed that "I just didn't know before I became a teacher. I just thought you put your lesson plan together in the morning, and you teach or whatever. And that's it. Right? But there's a lot of external stuff that student teachers don't get to consider" (2020 Research Interview).

The Early Years. The first few years of a teaching career are simultaneously exciting and intense. They are a formative period that heavily determines whether people remain in teaching and if so, "what kind of teacher they become" (Feiman-Nemser, 2001, p. 1026). These early years are also especially vulnerable because many teacher evaluation policies expect novices to demonstrate skills and abilities that they can only gain through experience (Dell'Angelo, 2021).

Year One. The steep learning curve of early career teaching (Darling-Hammond, 2010; Ro, 2019) is unavoidable, and the first year is often the most challenging part of a teacher's career. First-year teachers experience a reality shock as they are simultaneously teaching and still *learning to teach* while acclimating to their new school and community context (Feiman-Nemser, 2001; Hewett, 2019). In tandem, the first year is also an exciting time because it's a teacher's first opportunity to build their own classroom environment and attempt to make their visions of teaching a reality.

The simultaneous struggles and exhilaration of 1st-year teaching are an emotional whirlwind. For instance, an extensive 1990 study of nearly 1,500 1st-year teachers by Ellen Moir, founder of the New Teacher Center, established that participants experienced conflicting emotions ranging from anticipation, survival, and disillusionment to rejuvenation and reflection. While the teaching landscape has evolved over the last 30 years, 1st-year teachers today still experience similar ebbs and flows (French, 2018; Giboney Wall, 2016). The emotional roller coaster depicted in Figure 3.1 is helpful for understanding and mentoring 1st-year teachers.

While the challenges are immense, when primed to thrive, teachers end their first year feeling accomplished, reflective, and eager for year two—after a well-deserved summer break!

Years Two and Three. According to teacher development frameworks, 2nd- and 3rd-year teachers often continue to vacillate between survival and discovery mode (Huberman, 1993). Thus, many of the emotions experienced in year one will still surface but can be less intense. Second- and 3rd-year teachers continue to prioritize their own professional needs with specific attention to classroom management, curriculum mastery, and content delivery. These early career teachers tend to gain more confidence in their teaching abilities and capacity to juggle the multifaceted context of their professional role.

Figure 3.1. Phases of 1st-Year Teachers' Attitudes Toward Teaching

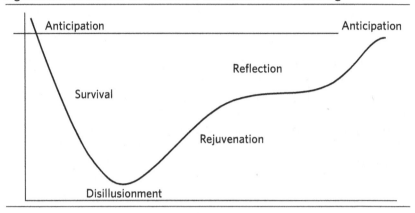

Some 2nd- and 3rd-year teachers begin to engage in broader school initiatives such as leading student clubs, coaching athletics, and more.

SUPPORTING PRESERVICE AND EARLY CAREER TEACHERS: A DEVELOPMENTAL APPROACH

Now that I have offered a glimpse into the ebbs and flows of early career teaching, let's turn to tools you can implement to support teachers during this foundational period. This section will share three activities that have resonated with my preservice and early career teacher participants: an interactive lecture, a teacher development reflection activity, and a 5-year goal-setting exercise. While there are many other innovative ways to tackle this topic, these are the three that have stood out over time.

Making Teacher Development Transparent Lecture

To prime teachers to thrive, it is crucial that they have a clear-eyed understanding of the teacher life cycle and understand that learning to teach is a process. With this understanding, new teachers are less likely to be too hard on themselves as they navigate the early career learning curve. These understandings can inspire them to adopt a growth mindset and display resilience toward their professional development. Concurrently, from an equity standpoint, pulling back the curtain of teacher development makes this nuanced process transparent.

Teaching Is Developmental

Figure 3.2. The Teacher Life Cycle

Novice	Apprentice	Professional	Expert	Distinguished	Emeritus
• Student Teaching	• First 1–3ish years	• 3rd–15ish years	• 12th–20ish years	• 10th–20+ years • Formal Recognition	• Retired, but still engaged

Note. Adapted from Steffy et al. (2000).

Transparency can help humanize novice teachers and show them that it is typical to struggle to learn the ropes. Hence, I propose that the first step is to deliberately educate preservice and early career teachers about the phases of teacher development. While there are many teacher development models, I find Steffy (2000) and colleagues' Life Cycle Model for Career Teachers especially helpful. Rather than the three broad life cycle phases agreed on in the literature (Coutler & Lester, 2011; Eros, 2011), Steffy and team proposed six phases of teacher development, as shown in Figure 3.2.

For a novice teaching audience, I focus on the first three phases. I typically begin with a short, interactive lecture introducing the topic of teacher development. I start with an overview that includes the image in Figure 3.2 and then discuss the following phase indicators, synthesized from Steffy et al. (2000) and other life cycle scholars (e.g., Christensen & Fessler, 1992; Huberman, 1993; Kelchtermans, 2017). Finally, I like to project and talk through these three phases on slides and/or provide them on a handout as shown in Figure 3.3.

After considering trends from this phase of teacher development, I ask participants to identify and discuss points that resonate with them. I also ask them to reflect on other experiences and emotions that complement or deviate from these themes. When I have preservice and early career teachers in the room together, I have found that it's fruitful to invite the more experienced participants to reminisce about their student teaching and share how they have evolved since this stage. This simultaneously helps early career teachers acknowledge their progress and reiterates to preservice teachers that the learning curve they are—and will be—experiencing is normal. Then we repeat this discussion process with an overview of the next stage as depicted in Figure 3.4.

Next, I like to examine what Steffy and colleagues (2000) named the "professional phase" of the teacher life cycle as shown in Figure 3.5. My goal is to communicate to preservice and early career teachers that

Figure 3.3. The Novice Phase: Student Teaching

To thrive during this phase, it is important to understand that:

1. This is the *exploration* phase of teaching:
   - Novice teachers are beginning to make sense of their professional identity.
   - Student teaching is an opportunity to take risks and learn through trial and error. A growth mindset is key!
2. Novice teachers are likely to have their idealism tested for the first time due to:
   - The clash between teacher preparation coursework focused on "best practices" and their schools' *actual* practices.
   - Feeling overwhelmed by the multiple tasks that come with student teaching.
   - Experiencing a range of conflicting emotions including anxiety, frustration, disillusionment, elation, fear, insecurity, and more.
3. Novice teachers' focus is on mastering lesson design and delivery:
   - At the same time, they should pay attention to the organizational, administrative, and interpersonal factors that teachers in their school juggle. Student teachers are likely not directly responsible for these parts of the job, but it's smart to have them on their radar.
   - Novice teachers are likely to struggle balancing the competing demands that professional teachers juggle.

Figure 3.4. The Apprentice Phase: The First Few Years

To thrive during this phase, it is important to understand that:

1. This is the most *complex* intellectual and emotional transition in the teacher life cycle. Apprentice teachers should give themselves grace!
2. It is typical to feel a sense of simultaneous survival and discovery.
3. Apprentice teachers are often laser focused on classroom management, curriculum mastery, and content delivery. Stay focused on mastering these important skills!

Apprentice teachers often navigate three common challenges:

1. Meeting personal and professional needs:
   - They want to be respected by colleagues.
   - They want to feel competent at their job.
   - They are navigating a whirlwind of emotions that can include feeling overwhelmed, discouraged, anxious, exhausted, depressed, uncertain, excited, and rewarded.
2. A reality shock:
   - Many 1st-year apprentice teachers are adjusting from the cooperating teacher support they likely had during student teaching.

(continued)

Figure 3.4. (*continued*)

- It's common to underestimate the time commitment of meeting multiple duties: juggling planning and instructional delivery, student assessment, classroom management, induction, professional development, state testing accountability measures, and more.
- This phase can feel overwhelming. This sentiment is normal. Things get easier over time!

3. Boundaries:
- Apprentice teachers are often tempted and even encouraged to engage in broader school initiatives such as extracurricular clubs, leadership roles, and so on.
- Apprentice teachers should set and stick to clear boundaries so that they have the time and space to find their groove in their classroom!
- School administrators and mentors should encourage and support apprentice teachers to set realistic boundaries. In fact, "attending to one's own pedagogical garden" (Huberman, 1993) by focusing on experimenting with classroom practices, new materials, and various student groupings can foster early career satisfaction and student achievement.

Figure 3.5. The Professional Phase: Over the Hump!

To thrive during this phase, it is important to understand that:

1. Professional teachers will have figured out their personal needs in the classroom, leaving space to focus on student needs.
2. Professional teachers will have increased self-confidence:
   - Confidence often reinvigorates their commitment to the profession;
   - A renewed commitment can fill teachers with more emotional and mental energy.
3. Professional teachers will have greater command of their pedagogy:
   - Instruction becomes a *living process* at this phase.
   - This is known as a "stabilization phase" where after lots of trial and error, teachers begin to consolidate their pedagogical repertoire. Professional teachers have figured out what works for them and their students!
4. Professional teachers have learned how to navigate the education system including school and district protocols.
5. Professional teachers are in a phase of continuous growth seeking. They often see themselves as lifelong learners.
6. Professional teachers have likely established a network of supportive colleagues.
7. Professional teachers may be comfortably taking on leadership roles, including mentoring student teachers, early career teachers, peer coaching, and more.

this next period is within reach and will be a phase when all their hard work pays off! As we process through this phase, I like to invite more experienced participants to share some of the indicators that they feel they have within reach. I also often prompt teachers to think about more experienced teachers they admire and discuss what they notice about these professional teachers in comparison to the teacher development indicators I share. It is often helpful to encourage teachers to find an opportunity to talk with teachers in the professional phase and ask them about their developmental trajectory and how they currently manage their time, personal, professional, and student needs.

Personal Reflection on Teacher Development

Following our interactive lecture described above, or if shared in a different manner, such as a handout, a quiet opportunity for personal reflection is fruitful. My participants keep a reflection journal where they can write and/or visually represent their thoughts on the reflection prompts that follow. Another option is to pair up and discuss the prompts. I often start with a time for personal journaling followed by time for partners to share. This allows everyone an opportunity to process independently and with a trusted peer. I typically have participants ponder the following questions shown in Figure 3.6.

Early Career Goal Setting

My early career participants and I have found the goal-setting exercise shown in Figure 3.7 impactful in helping them recognize that learning to teach is a developmental process. I typically have participants record their initial thinking in their reflection journal followed by paired or small group dialogue. Like the reflection activity above,

Figure 3.6. Early Career Development Reflection Prompts

1. What phase in the early career life cycle would you currently place yourself in? Why?
2. As you plan to thrive professionally, what aspects of the career life cycle do you need to keep in mind?
3. What actions can you take to support your thrival in the immediate to near future? What steps will require you to think big picture?

Figure 3.7. Goal Setting: Backward Mapping the First 5 Years

Keeping the early career teacher life cycle in mind and your ultimate why:[1]

1. Imagine the teacher you aspire to be in 5 years. Write about the following prompts that resonate with you:
   a. What do you know, understand, and do at this stage in your career?
   b. What will it feel like for students to be in your classroom?
   c. What do students, parents/guardians, colleagues, and administrators admire about you?
   d. How are you living out your ultimate why?
2. With this target in mind, backward map three to five incremental goals for each year, starting with year five.
   a. What steps can you take each year to achieve your 5th-year goals?
   b. What support do you need to get there? (This could be mentorship, colleagues, professional development, self-care, etc.)
3. How will you hold yourself accountable to your goals?

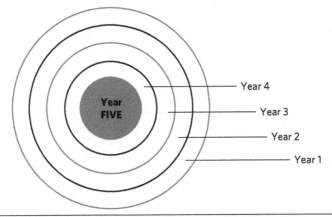

[1]Topic covered in prior chapter.

I try to allow time for personal journaling and paired dialogue. When time is short, I have found that this can be a great take-home activity that we can then revisit either in pairs, as a whole group, or virtually.

Several of the early career teachers I follow enthusiastically recall that this activity resonated with them and supported their resilience as they navigated their early career learning curve. For instance, 2nd-year teacher Mary reminisced that completing this exercise during her preservice program continues to help her "maintain perspective and remember that I will get better and better year by year. Focusing on

Figure 3.8. Chapter 3 Suggestions on How to Incorporate These Tools

Teacher Educators:
- Offer a workshop on this topic.
- Incorporate these tools into your teacher preparation program's orientation and written materials.
- Share the life cycle phases with cooperating teachers and student teaching supervisors. Encourage them to keep the early career life cycle phases in mind as they interact with and support preservice teachers.
- Infuse into your coursework. If you are short on time, assign all or parts of the provided tools as homework followed by an opportunity to debrief either in person or via an online discussion board.

Mentors:
- Incorporate this lecture and activities into your teacher induction professional development sessions. This could be presented live, as virtual recorded materials, or in a hybrid fashion.
- Incorporate the phases in one-on-one or small group discussions with early career teachers you support.
- Use this information to assess your mentee's life cycle phase and to advocate for developmentally appropriate professional expectations of early career teachers in your school and/or district.

New Teachers:
- Self-assess your current phase and revisit periodically. I recommend keeping an early career journal to process your development, reflect on, and celebrate your progress. It's also rewarding to look back over time and see how far you've come!
- Discuss these phases and reflection prompts in a book club with other early career teachers. Share your experiences, emotions, and insights.
- As emphasized in the early career phases, give yourself permission to focus on your classroom right now. Prioritize your classroom environment, building relationships with your students, planning lessons, and instructional delivery. Don't be afraid to set healthy boundaries!

annual baby steps helps me stay grounded. Right now, I'm just trying my best and failing a lot, but getting back up and trying again!"

INSIGHTS FROM PRESERVICE AND EARLY CAREER TEACHERS

As the saying goes, "knowledge is power." In this spirit, 1st-year teacher Maria wrote in her reflection journal, "this [our session about the teacher life cycle] oddly makes me feel better. The struggle is real.

I feel better and affirmed that I am doing the right thing." In fact, over the years, my early career participants consistently ruminated that understanding the teacher development phases illuminated the importance of being patient with themselves and seeking out community to thrive—lessons that can support their resilience.

Practicing Patience

Preservice teacher participants who were student teaching during our life cycle workshop recognized that a growth mindset, or as Casey put it, "a mindset of always learning," will help them maintain perspective and support resilience as they navigate the early learning curve. For instance, Jeffrey acknowledged that "becoming a strong teacher won't happen in a year or two; it takes time and dedication." Similarly, Jasmine recognized the importance of taking time to "notice and reflect on successes instead of just failures." Nikki reflected that "I need just to keep reminding myself that feeling secure will take time, and I must be patient with that. I am one of those people that tends to quit when I don't see instantaneous results. This is a habit I will have to get over to thrive."

First-year teacher participants shared similar insights. As Denise put it, examining the early career life cycle reminded her that "I will grow over time, and the challenges I am experiencing right now are not forever." Similarly, it was common for 1st-year teachers to acknowledge that "change is slow" and understanding the life cycle is a helpful "reminder of the teacher that I can become in time."

Second- and 3rd-year teachers noted their progress since beginning their careers. When James compared his first year to his second, he noticed that as a 2nd-year teacher, he was "able to focus on specific things rather than just trying to get through the day." Second- and 3rd-year teachers acknowledged that "teaching is fluid" and that thriving is a "continuum." Summer wrote, "I will toggle back and forth between stages as my journey continues." And Mike reflected that "learning is hard, [but] there will always be room for growth. Don't just focus on the bad things. Look at how you have grown. It takes time. Remember why you are here."

Thriving in Community

While embracing patience, participants also acknowledged the importance of community and mentorship. As they anticipated their first teaching jobs, preservice teachers hoped to seek out a positive support system. Carter wrote, "finding others who are passionate about learning and growing themselves for the good of their students is key." Moreover, preservice teachers hoped for guidance and mentorship. For instance, pondering finding her first job, Jasmine emphasized her desire to "find a community and teammates who have made it through many years and can be an emotional support and professional mentor to me."

Likewise, 1st-year teachers acknowledged the importance of asking for help, seeking out and "learning from mentor feedback." For example, Catherine reflected the importance of "knowing that it is okay to ask for help and that feedback means they care about you and want you to succeed, not that they think they are better than you." Likewise, her 1st-year peers recognized that acknowledging their vulnerabilities and seeking support from more experienced teachers, mentors, and administrators was essential.

While preservice and 1st-year teachers most frequently recognized the importance of mentorship, 2nd- and 3rd-year participants viewed like-minded peers as contributing to their ability to flourish. These experienced early career teachers emphasized seeking out positive colleagues. For example, Layla wrote that "surrounding myself with positivity is what I hold most dear." Similarly, Aubrey wrote that "collaborating and being creative with other teachers or people in the community" keeps her going. She concluded that "thriving does not happen in isolation." Finally, Katherine synthesized our session on teacher development like this:

> I think the big picture thing to remember is that each year gets better. Even with switching schools, moving across the country, having a quarter-life crisis, and surviving a global pandemic, the knowledge that things will improve is a huge relief. The information we looked at today was very helpful because it reminded me of the skills I have developed at this point in my career. It also reminded me of what all I've already gone through in terms of early-career struggles. Reflecting on how far I've come has been joyful!

CONCLUSION: RESILIENCE AND THE EARLY CAREER TEACHER LIFE CYCLE

Like Liz, whom we met at the beginning of this chapter, it is normal for new teachers to experience a reality shock as they learn the ropes. It is also normal for new teachers to wrestle with a whirlwind of emotions as they make sense of this complex profession. However, if we don't talk about these experiences with them and normalize the learning curve that accompanies becoming a teacher, we risk new teachers feeling alone and deflated. When new teachers feel isolated and discouraged, they may be less likely to reach out for support and more likely to conclude that they are not cut out to be teachers. Instead, being transparent with novices about the developmental phases they will experience can encourage their resilience and support them in embracing learning to teach as a lifelong, multifaceted, and joyous journey! Furthermore, the 5-year backward mapping activity featured in this chapter encourages novice teachers to set incremental goals and engage in ongoing praxis. By breaking down their career goals, beginning teachers may realize that becoming a master teacher takes time. Moving forward, I highly encourage teacher educators and early career mentors to keep the development phases at the forefront of their programming. Equitable teacher support requires humanizing preservice and early career teachers by acknowledging that learning to teach is a developmental and lifelong endeavor. With patience, peer and mentor guidance, determination, and practice, passionate early career teachers can flourish!

CHAPTER 4

Conflict Is Inevitable

Novice Teacher Agency to Navigate Tension

When you avoid conflict to make peace with other people, you start
a war within.

—Brené Brown

> **CHAPTER 4 GOALS**
>
> 1. For readers to understand the types and sources of conflict early
>   career teachers often experience
> 2. To provide readers with tools designed to empower preservice
>   and early career teachers to recognize and handle conflict in
>   healthy and productive ways
> 3. To share encouraging insights from preservice through 3rd-year
>   teachers who participated in the navigating conflict teacher
>   development exercises I detail

JENNA FACES TENSION WITH HER VETERAN COLLEAGUES

As a 1st-year teacher, most of Jenna's colleagues had worked at their
middle school since it opened 15 years ago. Due to her knowledge
of and commitment to supporting English language learners, a pop-
ulation that was quickly growing in their school and district, her
principal—who was also newer to the building—was excited to hire
Jenna. As the newest member of a three-person 6th-grade team, Jenna
was eager to collaborate on curriculum planning with her colleagues.
But she quickly learned that her English Language Arts teammates
were "opposed" to Jenna's suggestions and to the recent overall district emphasis on culturally responsive teaching. Team planning felt

"tense" to Jenna. Her colleagues "shut down" her suggestions during planning meetings. As a newer, younger teacher, Jenna felt intimidated by her colleagues and forced to comply with their ways:

> I felt so frustrated that for a brief time, I didn't see myself going back to the school. I was forced to teach something that I didn't want to. And to be lockstep, and doing material that I wasn't creating, and teaching materials that the kids hated. They hated that unit. And it killed me every single day. And that's the only time that I ended up really breaking down over feeling so out of control and the least amount of passion that I've felt in the classroom.

Luckily, at the end of the first semester, Jenna had the agency to share her feelings with her building principal and instructional coach. Together, they devised a plan to ensure Jenna's expertise was honored and her team included her ideas. While Jenna had to compromise with her colleagues on curriculum planning, she had administrative support to adapt her lessons to "motivate her students better." And, while it took time and collegial tension "would come and go," by her second year, her colleagues started to come around and open their minds to district changes. Eventually, one of her teammates voluntarily came to Jenna for ideas and even started sharing materials he gathered in professional development (Research Interviews, 2020 & 2021).

The insights and activities below came in handy as Jenna and other early career teachers learned to navigate professional conflict so they could flourish!

* * *

Interpersonal relationships are at the heart of teaching. In addition to students, novice teachers must learn to manage relationships with supervisors, colleagues, and families. As Jenna quickly learned, the interpersonal nature of education makes conflict an unavoidable aspect of the job. According to Bryan Harris, author of the book *17 Things Resilient Teachers Do: And 4 Things They Hardly Ever Do* (2021), conflict "is simply a byproduct of being around other people" (p. 103). However, many new teachers feel timid and unequipped to navigate school-related conflicts. While teacher preparation programs teach classroom management skills, which can help novices learn to navigate student-related conflict, it is rare that we explicitly focus on adult dynamics. But since Harris (2021) claims that resilient teachers "rarely shy away from conflict" (p. 102), it is vital to equip novice teachers with the tools and agency to anticipate and handle professional tension and conflict effectively. Hence, this chapter aims to familiarize readers with how various education stakeholders can be a source of conflict; common tensions that arise, including intergenerational and interracial tensions; and why it's essential to acknowledge and proactively resolve conflict. Finally, I share tools for novice teachers to navigate tension and conflict so they can advocate for equity and thrive!

CONFLICT AT SCHOOL

School leadership, colleagues, and parents/guardians are all sources of potential conflict for new teachers. As discussed in Chapter 1, school climate plays a significant role in novice teachers' capacity to thrive. An effective school leader fosters a positive school climate. In this vein, a good administrator creates an environment that manages conflict in a healthy manner, recognizes tensions between stakeholders, and monitors and/or intervenes appropriately. For instance, a 2019 case study by Vuyisile Msila closely studied two schools, one with an administrator who adopted a healthy approach to conflict management and another with a principal who had an unhealthy approach. Msila found that conflict management played a crucial role in the former school's success and the latter's lack of success. When school leaders manage conflict effectively, tensions can lead to positive outcomes, including personal and collective growth (Harris, 2021). Hence, novice teachers should seek out schools whose leaders have a proactive and robust approach to conflict management. In this vein, when my team and I guide teacher candidates through the job-search process, we encourage them to directly ask potential employees how they address conflict between teachers and administration, colleagues, and families. Employers who can easily answer this question with concrete examples are more likely to have established healthy conflict management routines in their school culture.

Along with administrators, colleagues can be an essential source of a new teacher's job satisfaction. Positive and productive collegial relationships help teachers manage their work-related stress, whereas hostile relationships can lead to burnout and attrition (Buchanan et al., 2013; Gavish & Friedman, 2010; Marcionetti & Castelli, 2022). Studies indicate that sometimes new teachers feel excluded by their more experienced colleagues (Farrell, 2016; Romero, 2021). Competitive and individualistic school cultures are sources of exclusion. For instance, sometimes more experienced teachers are not welcoming to those with less experience, leaving novices to feel isolated and vulnerable (Farrell, 2016; Romero, 2021). Romero (2021) studied new teachers who solved feelings of isolation in their grade level or departmental teams by seeking alternative collegial communities. These teachers collaborated with other new colleagues outside their grade level or discipline. These newly formed communities of practice helped members not only survive but thrive in their schools.

Parents and guardians are a child's first and most important teachers. Culturally sustaining partnerships with families increase student achievement and overall well-being (Herrera et al., 2020; Powell & Rightmyer, 2011). At the same time, tensions between teachers and parents/guardians can occur. Family–school tension and conflict occur for a variety of reasons (Epstein, 2018; Zeichner, 2022), including the following:

- Miscommunication or poor communication
- Cultural and linguistic differences
- Deficit views of minoritized families
- Lack of trust
- Parents/guardians who are, or are perceived as, overly demanding
- Parents/guardians' negative experiences in their K–12 schooling

Yet thriving teachers are proactive, compassionate, reflexive, and deliberate about communication and relationship building with parents and guardians (Herrera et al., 2020; Nordell, 2021).

Typical Teacher Tensions

Since they are new to their career and getting to know an unfamiliar school environment, novice teachers are especially vulnerable when it comes to work-related conflict. Differences in beliefs and values, generational tension, and workplace bullying are frequent, and sometimes intersecting, sources of school-based interpersonal conflict (Vilar et al., 2016).

Conflicting Beliefs and Values. One of the most common sources of work-related tension is differences in the beliefs and values of novice teachers, their more experienced colleagues, and/or administration (Vilar et al., 2016). As discussed in Chapter 2, new teachers are typically most motivated by the profession's altruistic, intrinsic, and/or spiritual aspects—they identify as role models and change makers. For instance, the novice teachers I feature in this book, such as Jenna, value culturally sustaining pedagogy. This priority requires teachers to commit to critical consciousness to guide curriculum and instruction, assessments, and their overall professional priorities. However, public schools are pressured to prioritize academic performance, primarily measured by test scores—measures that are not holistically able to assess student achievement from a lens of equity and inclusion. These pressures lead to prioritizing external motivators over the intrinsic and altruistic reasons that draw many people into the profession. This can cause friction with teachers' core values, which often leads to pedagogical and curricular conundrums. For instance, administrative or collegial pressures to "teach to the test" can compel novices to alter or abandon the research-based teaching methods they studied and valued in their teacher training (Farrell, 2016; Romero, 2021).

Generational Tension. Generational tension is another common source of conflict novice teachers are likely to encounter. According to Lyons and colleagues (2015), our current workforce includes members of four distinct generations known as baby boomers, Generation X, millennials, and Generation Z. As these generations interact, they form perceptions of each other's expectations, values, work ethic, and more. These perceptions can lead to stereotypes, preconceptions, and intergenerational tension (Finkelstein et al., 2013; Gill, 2002). For example, it is common in U.S. media and pop culture to stereotype Generation X as cynical and Generation Z as civic-minded. The literature suggests that newer teachers, especially younger new teachers, can feel excluded by and vulnerable around their more experienced colleagues (Farrell, 2016; Romero, 2021). These feelings can perpetuate stereotypes, preconceptions, and intergenerational friction.

Workplace Bullying. Workplace bullying is another possible source of distress and conflict. Bullying is defined as a recursive pattern of hostile behaviors where the bully, typically a supervisor or more experienced colleague, exploits their power over subordinates (Cowie et al., 2002; Yadav et al., 2020). For instance, in my first teaching assignment, there was a veteran teacher bully whose behavior was contagious. She would often comment on newer teachers' arrival and departure times (insinuating we were not working enough), gossip about colleagues and administration, mock parents, and intimidate her colleagues into not adopting curricular changes. Over time, several other teachers adopted her actions, contributing to a toxic school climate. To preserve my integrity, I avoided the staff lounge and voluntarily relocated to a mobile classroom where I could circumvent as much toxicity as possible. In another teaching assignment, our school principal was a bully who exerted her power to intimidate and threaten teachers who asked questions or pushed back on hierarchical decisions. Everyone felt like they were constantly walking on eggshells—another example of a toxic work environment. Both situations increased my stress and hindered my ability to thrive. Unsurprisingly, research shows that teachers who are victims of workplace bullying experience a decrease in their well-being, increased absenteeism, decreased work performance, reduced job satisfaction, and are more likely to quit. Workplace bullying harms the victim, and the entire school can experience a loss of morale, productivity, and institutional knowledge (Cabrera, 2013; Yadav et al., 2020).

Avoiding Conflict Equates to Eluding Equity

On top of tensions around values, between generations, and stressors of workplace bullying, conflict avoidance is another prominent barrier to thriving. Many people are socialized to evade conflict—especially when it comes to acknowledging and working across differences. So, while it's important that budding teachers and their mentors understand sources of tension, it is equally necessary that we learn how to navigate conflict in culturally sustaining and humanizing ways.

Given that my teacher preparation program and many other programs are committed to culturally sustaining practices, novice teachers need to understand how dominant members of society (in my case the United States), including many educators, tend to deal with conflict in unproductive and oppressive ways. One common way many teachers are socialized to handle tension and conflict is through the construct of whiteness. Whiteness refers to the social construction of the white race, white culture, ideologies, and the systems of power and privilege afforded to white-skinned people through daily life, including, but not limited, to policies, media, decision-making power, the judicial system, and education (Bonilla-Silva, 2006; Helms, 1990; Leonardo, 2009).

People in the United States and other westernized countries, regardless of racial or ethnic identity, can be socialized into and can perform whiteness (Fasching-Varner, 2013). Education scholars have found that whiteness is often performed through "niceness" (Fasching-Varner, 2013; Gardiner et al., 2022). "Whiteness as niceness" is the assumption that being pleasant and kind is how to "not be racist." Moreover, this performance of niceness is surface level, conflict averse, and doesn't foster positive change. This is especially common regarding uncomfortable dialogue about race and inequity where those performing whiteness may claim they are race- or colorblind or become easily defensive during conversations around difference. Yet we cannot change oppressive systems without acknowledgment of difference and productive conversations about them. If we are committed to change, we must lean into discomfort!

Many people, including novice teachers, are afraid of not being liked or being viewed negatively if they acknowledge and talk about uncomfortable topics, including race, gender, sexuality, disability, and other politically loaded topics. This resistance to, or avoidance of, challenging dialogue perpetuates educational inequities. If we don't engage in productive dialogue, we cannot understand, respect, heal from, and change racial, ethnic, and other oppressive divides (Sue, 2015; Whitaker & Valtierra, 2019).

In his book *Race Talk and the Conspiracy of Silence,* Dareld Wing Sue (2015) asserts that there are three reasons people, including educators, are socialized to avoid or disrupt uncomfortable conversations about race:

1. *The politeness protocol:* Akin to whiteness as niceness, the politeness protocol is a socialized "ground rule" that potentially offensive or uncomfortable topics should be avoided, silenced, or spoken about only in a very light, superficial manner—especially in diverse contexts (Sue, p. 24–25).
2. *The colorblind protocol:* Colorblindness became popular around the 1960s civil rights era. The colorblind protocol is the false idea that one way not to be perceived as racist is by not acknowledging race, racism, and difference. The reality is

that we *do* perceive differences, so pretending that we don't is highly problematic.
3. *The academic protocol:* This is a false idea that teaching and learning are objective; therefore, personal experiences and emotions do not have a place in schooling. Being labeled as different, experiencing inequity, and systemic racism are emotional and personal. We reproduce systemic oppression when we don't honor, acknowledge, and learn from personal feelings and stories.

Educators who adopt these problematic strategies will be unequipped to recognize, dialogue, and change the inequitable and oppressive nature of schooling (Kavanagh et al., 2021). In contrast, teachers who acknowledge these protocols and commit to resisting them are more likely to enact culturally sustaining practices. Therefore, to thrive as culturally sustaining teachers, we must lean into discomfort and dialogue about and across differences. We must be brave to thrive!

SUPPORTING PRESERVICE AND EARLY CAREER TEACHERS TO NAVIGATE CONFLICT

Over the years, I've found that it is vital to ensure teacher candidates know that tension and conflict are an inevitable part of the job. And equipping them with the tools to navigate conflict—including the unavoidable tensions that arise when acknowledging and learning to dismantle oppressive systems, including education—is essential to preparing them to thrive. So, my first step in supporting novice teachers to navigate tension and conflict is to share how it operates in schools, as outlined in the section above. Then I find it helpful to dig a little deeper into how people often experience conflict.

Mindfulness and Stories of Tension

Since the academic protocol perpetuates inequity, I find it helpful to leverage personal stories. According to Connelly and Clandinin (2004), leaders in the field of narrative research, telling our stories is a salient means of understanding our experiences, other people's experiences, and the world. Hence, after an overview of the concepts discussed above, I ask teachers to consider their encounters with tension and conflict in schools. I've found that student teachers typically

Conflict Is Inevitable 69

have yet to experience much tension and conflict (at least when deliberately placed in a healthy school context). Hence, I often have more experienced teachers pair up with student teachers to share their stories. Then I usually pair up participants to dialogue as they share a relevant school conflict–related story they either experienced or witnessed. Next, I ask participants to pause and reflect on how recollecting the story felt in their physical bodies. In response, participants share physical sensations that typically include feelings such as a racing heart, clenching jaw, tightness in the chest, neck, shoulders and more.

Next, I ask participants to share emotions that the story brought up. Typical responses include feelings of stress, anxiety, anger, fear, and more. I emphasize that recognizing and acknowledging these physical and emotional sensations helps move through the feelings that conflict triggers (Jennings, 2015). And with practice, this mindfulness approach allows our brains to recognize and know how to respond to sensations more efficiently (Gibson, 2019). Next, I share the insights that follow in Figure 4.1 on a slide and/or handout.

Finally, I have participants revisit their stories and determine whether they experienced the scenario from a cognitive stance, affective stance, or a little bit of both. After participants have categorized their conflict, I share the insights about conflict and control

Figure 4.1. How Conflict Operates

1. **Conflict signals the brain to shift into *survival mode*.** This makes the brain *hyper-focus* its attention on the conflict. Conflict is emotional.
2. **Conflict can be healthy, and conflict can be unhealthy.**
   - **Cognitive** conflict can be healthy.
     - » This is when we disagree about issues, ideas, and/or processes.
     - » Cognitive conflict can be productive because it challenges our beliefs, can push us to improve, and is focused on the what, why, and how of an important issue.
     - » Cognitive conflict responses can include collaboration, accommodation, and compromise.
   - **Affective** conflict is often unhealthy.
     - » This is when we hold grudges and focus on past experiences and emotions centered around people and events.
     - » Affective conflict reactions can include competition, avoidance, and complaining.

Note. Adapted from Harris (2021), Mamiya et al. (2020), and Thomas & Kilman, 1978.

Figure 4.2. Conflict: Leverage What You Can Control

As teachers, we must personify our responsibilities as **leaders** and **role models**. Therefore:

1. Try **not to take conflict personally**.
2. Be **responsive** rather than reactive. It's best to try not to exacerbate tensions. Deal with them promptly.
3. **Separate the person from the problem**. This helps shift an affective conflict to one that is cognitive. Avoid pronouns. When we can remain neutral in our language, we are more likely to view the conflict from a cognitive stance.
4. Be **empathetic**. Remember, no one is ever 100% correct, and no one is ever 100% wrong. Everyone has their perception, which is their current reality.
5. Be **respectful**. Avoid exaggerating, sarcasm, trivializing, gossiping, and so on.
6. Be **courageous**. Self-awareness, self-love, and vulnerability are potent attributes of a brave leader and, therefore, a thriving teacher.
7. Keep our **ultimate why** at the forefront. Our why reflects our values. We must stay true to our values.

Note. Adapted from Brown (2018) and Harris(2021).

shown in Figure 4.2. I like to remind participants that these understandings are critical to embody with *all* stakeholders, including how they mitigate conflict with students since their job is to be a positive role model.

I typically present the insights above as a handout that participants can keep. In addition, since I use reflection journals, I usually have teachers attach this handout to their journals for future reference and take some time to journal about their strengths and areas for growth.

Practicing Productive Conflict Resolution

Another helpful exercise to support novice teachers' agency toward conflict is to role-play. In my workshops, we often prepare and then role-play how to effectively navigate a brave conversation with a person from the original story teachers shared in the exercise discussed above. Partners will often pick the most challenging of the two scenarios they discussed with their peers and then work together to script their framing of that conversation as depicted in Figure 4.3. As a stand-alone role-play activity, facilitators can also create scenarios for participants to work from.

Conflict Is Inevitable 71

Figure 4.3. Framing a Brave Conversation Template

Keep the following encouraging insight from Brené Brown (2018) in mind: Clear is KIND.

Say what you mean, and mean what you say.

Step 1: Name the issue: *I want to talk to you about the effect. . . . Or, I have noticed that. . .*

Step 2: Select a specific example that illustrates the behavior or situation you want to change. *For example. . .*

Step 3: Describe your emotions about this issue. *I feel. . . .*

Step 4: Name your values as they relate to this issue. *I value. . . . Or xxx is an essential value to me. . . . Or this classroom/our team/our school values. . . .*

Step 5: Clarify what is in jeopardy: *I want to share with you what is at stake. . . .*

Step 6: Identify and take responsibility for your contribution to the problem. *I recognize my contribution to this issue in that . . .*

Step 7: Indicate your wish to solve this issue: *I want to solve this issue together, the effect that (x is having on y). . . .*

Step 8: Invite your partner to respond: *I want to learn your perspective. What's going on from your viewpoint?*

Note. Adapted from *Fierce Conversations*, Susan Scott (2017, p. 203).

Finally, after pairs have scripted their brave conversation framing, we pick one to two scenarios that we collectively determine are most likely to occur—and workshop-potential best-case and/or worst-case conversations. Then, as a group—or in smaller teams when the group is large—we practice role-playing the scenarios using the following roles shown in Figure 4.4.

Role-playing can sometimes feel staged and a bit silly. However, I've found that leaning into humor and lightheartedness can remind participants that we are all in this together—it takes the edge off a common stressful reality. Moreover, the more we practice brave conversations, the more we flex those metaphorical muscles. While role-playing isn't the same as experiencing real conflict, it does allow us to proactively prepare for and reflect on how to navigate school-based tension productively. This can be empowering.

Figure 4.4. Brave Conversation Role-Play Fishbowl

Facilitator: The role-play guide. The facilitator helps organize roles and keeps the role-play moving in a productive direction.

Initiator: The teacher who initiates and frames the brave conversation. Initiator chooses the level of "challenge" they would like to experience in the conversation from a range of best-case response to a worst-case scenario. Then they practice initiating and navigating the brave conversation.

Responder: The person or people in the conflict responding to initiated conversation. This person takes on the level of challenge expressed by the initiator and role-plays a response to the initiator.

Friends to phone: These participants help the initiator and responder navigate and problem solve. Initiators and responders can pause at any point during the role-play to "phone a friend." Likewise, the session facilitator can pause when they recognize a teachable moment and facilitate team problem solving.

Notetakers: These participants take careful notes of the conversation. Notetakers will compare notes at the end of the scenario and share themes. The purpose is to mirror what happened in the role-play for collective reflection and feedback.

Timekeeper: This person tracks our agreed-on time limit and signals us throughout the role-play and when time is almost up.

Figure 4.5. Chapter 4 Suggestions on How to Incorporate These Tools

Teacher Educators:
- Be transparent that navigating tension and conflict are an inevitable part of the job. Start with educating teacher candidates about conflict in classroom management coursework. Then extend this to how to navigate conflict with supervisors, colleagues, and families.
- Incorporate these tools into relevant coursework and/or workshops. Be diligent about placing teacher candidates in a healthy and positive school environment. While schools are never perfect, teacher candidates need to experience what a well-functioning school looks like and feels like.
- When they begin the job search, support candidates to recognize the signs of a positive and toxic administrator and school climate. Help them recognize a school that aligns with their values and goals.

Mentors:
- Be transparent with novice teachers about the culture of your school and school district when it comes to navigating tension and conflict.
- Watch for unwelcoming behaviors and exclusion from other teachers.
- Remind teammates of the importance of and responsibility to collaborate with their novice colleagues.

(continued)

Conflict Is Inevitable   73

Figure 4.5. (*continued*)

- Educate more experienced colleagues about the importance of being inclusive of novices, how inclusion can mitigate turnover, and the weight of their positive leadership as experienced teachers on newer teachers.
- Act as a sounding board and support system for novice teachers as they encounter tension and conflict both in and out of the classroom. Add the topic of tension and conflict to your regularly scheduled check-ins. Remind them that these experiences are normal, and, with the right tools, they can get through it.
- Be an advocate and support system for your mentee if a conflict accelerates to a point where they need supervisor intervention.
- Incorporate this workshop and tools into induction programming. This could be presented live, as virtual recorded materials, or in a hybrid fashion.

New Teachers:
- Keep the recommendations from the exercises I share in a location where you can review them and practice them until they become habit.
- Lean on trusted mentors and other novice teachers to help you vent, process, problem solve, and workshop initiating brave conversations.
- Advocate for yourself. When conflict arises, which it will, frame it in accordance with your ultimate why and/or school values and commitments.
- Be proactive and remember that brave conversations tend to go more smoothly than we anticipate.
- Practice, practice, practice. Navigating tension and conflict productively is a like a muscle—the more you do it, the easier it becomes. It can help to script out the brave conversation before you initiate it.
- Brave conversations need to happen in person. Avoid engaging in conflict via email. This leads to miscommunication and perpetuates further conflict.

INSIGHTS FROM PRESERVICE AND EARLY CAREER TEACHERS

Early career teachers who participated in the exercises I describe above were able to reflect on the conflict-oriented challenges they experienced thus far and gained new insights and strategies that empowered them to navigate workplace conflict with confidence. In line with the research, a handful of the participants who were experiencing significant tension and conflict at school struggled with tension with their administration and/or colleagues (Farrell, 2016; Harris, 2021; Msila, 2019; Romero, 2021). These teachers most frequently reflected that clashing values and beliefs were a source of conflict (Harris, 2021). Differences in attitudes about curriculum, pedagogy, families, and culturally sustaining practices were frequent sources of tension for some of the participating teachers. Others indicated that mistrusting relationships were the source of their workplace tension. For some, their school principals were the direct source of distress, displaying poor communication, generational tension, or bullying. In other cases, colleagues were the most significant source of stress (Cowie et al., 2002; Finkelstein et al., 2013; Yadav et al., 2020).

Despite these barriers to thriving, there were three common ways that teacher participants anticipated navigating current and future school-related tension and conflict:

- A positive mindset
- Leaning on and forging strong staff relationships
- Initiating brave conversations

Thriving Through Tension

Novice teachers who have participated in my TTLC workshops recognize that staying rooted in their ultimate why, adopting a solution-oriented disposition, and having an optimistic mindset are strategies they have agency over to navigate tension and conflict. For instance, 1st-year teacher Denise noted that "staying centered and remembering why I do this job helps me not get caught up in the little things that could bring me down." And 2nd-year teacher Sara found success in "choosing my battles and bringing solutions when discussing problems" was a helpful attitude. Finally, Lexie, a 3rd-year teacher, noted, "as long as I don't get caught up internalizing negative energy, I think I'm good."

Unanimously, participants named like-minded colleagues and supportive administration as vital to their ability to flourish and productively handle tension. As Casey, a high school student teacher, put it, "people need other people, and this journey is much more enjoyable with a like-minded companion." Similarly, 3rd-year teacher Anna wrote, "Positive relationships are the key to thriving; you need to have positive relationships with staff, administration, and students, or else this job is just simply not for you. Teaching is a very social profession, and relationships are key to thriving."

Several teachers could name at least one amicable colleague they could lean on and collaborate with, or as 3rd-year teacher Aubrey put it, her "teacher bestie!" Furthermore, the teachers struggling to find supportive colleagues left the session motivated to build a network. As Carter, a high school student teacher, acknowledged, "So far, I've

Conflict Is Inevitable

been shy and, I think, not very confident in initiating relationships with the teaching staff. I am going to put myself out there and get to know the rest of the teachers. Relationships with kids are key, so it makes sense that building relationships with colleagues is also valuable." Other participants noted creative ways to find their people via networking through teacher-oriented social media platforms, expanding their outreach to other grade levels or disciplines, colleagues in neighboring schools, and/or our novice teacher learning community.

Like Jenna, whom we met at the opening of this chapter, supportive relationships with the administration are also essential. For example, 2nd-year teacher Jordan, whose school district was petitioning to remove several teacher planning days, noted, "I have to say that my principal really positively affected me when he went to bat for us teachers. . . . It felt rejuvenating to be heard." Furthermore, 2nd-year elementary school teacher Summer noted that her school climate was supportive, aligned, and she felt "part of a larger team." She appreciates her administration, which "makes me feel supported and defended when it comes to challenging students and parents. Overall, my admin works to support teachers in their personal and professional journeys, which helps me feel like I can grow and thrive."

Finally, participants recognized the value of initiating brave conversations when conflict arises. For instance, 1st-year elementary school teacher Maria reflected, "I am such a people pleaser at work . . . it's time to self-advocate and initiate meaningful dialogue . . . even though it's scary." Moreover, teachers acknowledged that change is inevitable and can trigger conflict. Third-year high school English teacher Aubrey noted that one tool to thrive is to "accept the changes that are to come and have honest conversations about what is expected." Furthermore, 1st-year elementary teacher Maria, a parent to two young children, role-played a courageous conversation with colleagues who "talk negatively of parents and in general see mal intent where there is none. In reality, we, as teachers, are surrounded by parents who, for the most part, just want the very best for the most special human being in the world to them." Maria was able to reframe family engagement in hopes of helping her non-parenting colleagues understand the positive intentions behind families' involvement. Finally, 2nd-year high school social studies teacher Anna reflected that to uphold her commitment to multicultural education, she must stay grounded in "truthful and holistic" education, despite related tensions from her more resistant colleagues. She planned to initiate a brave conversation, one we practiced in our role-play, with her departmental colleagues about how "omitting the true history of this country" is harmful. She also planned to offer to collaboratively design culturally sustaining lessons with her colleagues.

CONCLUSION: AGENCY AND COURAGE FOR DIALOGUE

If the current U.S. political climate indicates how our society copes with conflict, we don't handle it in productive, respectful, dignifying, or responsible ways. Contemporary political discourse is divisive and does not inspire the critical dialogue popular critical theorists like Paulo Freire (1970) and bell hooks (1994) argued is vital for social change. Moreover, scholars have found that divisiveness has inundated U.S. schools, including how some students, based on negative political discourse, are emboldened to bully, harass, and intimidate their minoritized peers (Au, 2017; Costello, 2016; Lombardo, 2019). Moreover, political divisiveness influences how some teachers negatively interact with minoritized students and colleagues (Kavanagh et al., 2021). Finally, other teachers feel threatened and silenced to speak up against hateful rhetoric (Cohen, 2022; Costello).

Teachers with the dispositions (Whitaker & Valtierra, 2019) and skills to deliver culturally responsive and sustaining pedagogy are powerful agents of social change. One important way to effect change is to ensure our newest generation of teachers learns how to navigate conflict. This requires that teacher preparation programs and early career mentors demystify the realities of interpersonal conflict that novice teachers are likely to experience. Teacher educators and early career mentors also have the collective responsibility to support them in handling conflict in proactive and productive ways. Finally, we must acknowledge that conflict is inevitable and, when navigated humanely, can foster positive personal and collective agency for change and growth. The chance to continuously evolve is how we flourish!

CHAPTER 5

Teacher Well-Being

Fueling Identity, Resilience, and Agency for Busy New Teachers

Self-care is not self-indulgence; it is self-preservation.

—Audre Lorde

CHAPTER 5 GOALS

1. For readers to understand the reasons novice teachers are at risk for excessive stress, anxiety, and other symptoms of negative well-being
2. To provide readers with tangible tools designed to help busy preservice and early career teachers to prioritize their well-being
3. To share encouraging insights from preservice through 3rd-year teachers who participated in the well-being exercises I detail

---

ANNA RECLAIMS A WELL-BEING ROUTINE

During her undergraduate degree and teacher training, Anna went to college on a cross-country scholarship. Consequently, she had a good routine for taking care of herself that encompassed daily training, nutrition, a mindfulness practice, and getting enough sleep. However, several of her well-being habits began to slip during her first 2 years as a middle school science teacher when she also became a new mom. She explained,

> I got to school by 6:30 most mornings and didn't leave until seven on the days I was coaching track. By the time I got home, I just wanted to shove whatever I could find into my mouth, play with the baby, and then

crawl into bed and binge something frivolous. . . . I told my husband, "If I can't do at least a 5-mile run, then what's the point?"

These changes in her habits took a toll on Anna's overall health and ability to cope with her anxiety, the day-to-day stress of teaching and parenting her daughter. She was ready to make a change for the better when she joined our TTLCs during the spring of her second year of teaching. When we met for coffee the following fall, Anna was excited to tell me that she had found a couple of small ways to bolster her well-being. While she no longer had time for long runs, she committed to coming to school later most mornings so she could take short runs while pushing her daughter in her stroller. She also started a new mindfulness habit of reflecting and setting daily intentions. She even started sharing her intentions with her students:

> Now, every morning during my run, I reflect on something. I do my intentions for the kids. Every day, I have intentions. And I set intentions for myself and tell them [students] the intentions. And so, that's the practice that I've done because I want them [students] to understand that it's good to reflect and to breathe.

As we chatted about her new habits, Anna mentioned that her next goal was to find efficient ways to cook healthy meals. She noted, "I already feel much better at managing stress, which is a major bonus, and they [her students] can tell too" (Research Interviews, 2019 & 2020).

What follows are insights and exercises that helped Anna and other novice teachers commit to their well-being despite being busy people who were navigating the early career teacher learning curve!

* * *

Teaching is a selfless act. Yet the reality is that if we don't deliberately care for ourselves, we can quickly become depleted and unable to give our students our best. Hence, as Kralovec and colleagues (2021) noted in their collection of K–12 educator essays on the topic of well-being, we must commit to "putting our oxygen mask on first" to fully care for our beloved students. However, it is common for new teachers, like Anna, to deprioritize their well-being while juggling the novice learning curve.

The American Psychological Association (APA, 2023) defines well-being as "a state of happiness and contentment, with low levels of distress, overall good physical and mental health and outlook, or good quality of life" (para 1). Self-care is a common way to attend to well-being. Mills and colleagues (2018) define self-care as "the self-initiated behavior that people choose to incorporate to promote good health and general wellbeing" (p. 1). They emphasize that while being healthy is an aspect of self-care, it's also about incorporating coping strategies to deal with stress.

This chapter begins with an overview of some of the ways new teachers' well-being is threatened. I then discuss ways that teachers, mentors and school leaders can support novice teacher well-being. Finally, I share tangible tools for busy novices to attend to their well-being and encouraging insights from teachers who participated in the strategies I share.

BEING NOVICE, BEING VULNERABLE

Teacher well-being is a real issue and one I experienced firsthand. As a new teacher, I learned the vital importance of attending to my well-being the hard way. Between learning classroom management, juggling multiple job expectations, and adapting to the constant and changing demands from my school district, I was overwhelmed and overworked. I ran myself ragged over the first few years. There wasn't much mainstream talk about self-care when I began my career, so I lacked the tools to attend to my well-being.

Being overworked in combination with a lack of knowledge about well-being and self-care resulted in emotional exhaustion, anxiety, panic attacks, and physical symptoms, including a nasty stress-induced rash that ran up my chest to my neck for months—Yuck! Since stress management is critical to a healthy immune system, I was frequently sick (Daugherty, 2019). I didn't know how to unplug, take time for myself, and separate myself from my work. By my third year, I had several panic attacks, which pushed me to learn how to prioritize my well-being.

Over the years, I have learned that I was not alone. Many novice teachers run themselves to the ground, which can contribute to burnout, physical illness, anxiety, depression, and more (Allies, 2021; Jennings, 2020). With teaching, we are constantly doing two things simultaneously: engaging in the act of teaching and learning *how* to teach (Jennings, 2020; Kralovec et al., 2021). As discussed in Chapter 3, we can only learn so much in teacher preparation (Clark, 2012; Feiman-Nemser, 2001). Studies show that acquiring the knowledge, skills, understanding, and intuition of an effective teacher typically takes about 5 years (Cuban, 2010, Ericsson et al., 2007). Furthermore, teachers—experienced and novice alike—are notoriously overstretched between curriculum planning, teaching students for 5–8 hours per day, assessment and grading, professional development, committee assignments, extracurricular commitments, collaborating with families and colleagues, performative reform pressures, and more.

Learning to juggle multiple and often conflicting responsibilities can cause new teachers to be overworked. And when we are overworked, it's common to neglect self-care. For instance, if a new teacher works 50–60 hours per week to meet all their obligations, they will lack time and energy for proper sleep, exercise, healthy eating, and other self-care. This makes them susceptible to depression, anxiety, emotional exhaustion, burnout, and physical illness.

The day-to-day workload, emotional labor that comes with working with youth, and top-down pressures mean that teachers are susceptible to depression and/or anxiety (Allies, 2021). According to the American Psychiatric Association (APA) (2013), symptoms of depression can include the following:

- Persistent fatigue
- Reduced engagement with others and/or activities
- The feeling of insignificance
- Diminished feelings of optimism

We experience anxiety through excessive worry or fear (APA). Depression and anxiety can often coexist, negatively affecting our overall well-being (McLean et al., 2020). When unattended, the emotional exhaustion that comes with teaching can lead to or add to depression, anxiety, and other negative emotional and physical symptoms (Chan et al., 2021). These symptoms negatively affect overall quality of life, relationships, work, and physical health. When teachers are struggling, it's hard to fully care for students.

Along with navigating the steep learning curve and juggling multiple and often conflicting job demands (Barkatsas & Malone, 2005;

Lim & Chai, 2008; Valtierra & Whitaker, 2021), novice teachers are especially vulnerable to negative mental and physical health symptoms for a few reasons.

1. **Demanding Classroom Environments:** It is common for administrators to put novice teachers in the most challenging assignments despite their being the least prepared to meet these demands (Bieler et al., 2016). School leaders often assign new teachers more class preparations, lower-achieving students, more students experiencing adversity (McLean et al., 2020), and more behaviorally challenged students than their experienced colleagues (Grissom et al., 2015). Furthermore, new teachers are prone to emotional exhaustion and burnout if school leaders do not support them in mitigating challenging student behaviors (Clercq et al., 2022).

2. **Job Ambiguity:** When teachers are new to a school, it takes time to understand the nuanced expectations of the job, especially if they are not explicitly spelled out by mentors and administrators (Boogren, 2021). The multiple and often conflicting demands of teaching can contribute to poor novice teacher well-being (De Clercq et al., 2022). While some ambiguity can be positive and lead us to exercise our professional autonomy, excessive amounts can lead to stress and anxiety.

3. **Teacher Evaluation Processes:** New teachers are often expected to perform like their more experienced colleagues, even though they are still learning (Feiman-Nemser, 2001, McMahon et al., 2015; TeKippe et al., 2020). These unrealistic top-down expectations are a significant source of teacher distress. Anderson and colleagues (2019) examined the perceptions of 1,274 Michigan teachers and their administrators on the relationships between the teacher evaluation process and teacher well-being. They found that teachers and administrators had notably different perceptions of how the evaluation process either supported or harmed teacher well-being. While teachers felt that the evaluation process negatively affected their well-being, administrators perceived that the process increased it. In contrast to their administrators, teachers in the study reported that evaluation pressures contributed to unhealthy competition between colleagues, administrator inconsistency, and overall stress.

WHAT WORKS

Luckily, there are many ways that teachers, their mentors, and school leaders can support novice teacher well-being. Two of the most important things teachers can do are to prioritize their physiological needs and engage in mindfulness (Allies, 2021; Boogren, 2018). Foremost, new teachers should focus on their hierarchy of needs (Maslow, 1943, 1972). At our most basic level, attending to our physiological needs such as getting plenty of rest, hydration, and healthy food is an important act of self-care that many busy new teachers neglect (Boogren, 2018). Furthermore, novice teachers can engage in mindfulness both inside and outside of their workday. Put simply, mindfulness is a nonsecular, nonjudgmental conscious process of observing our thoughts and feelings. Mindfulness supports emotional regulation, empathy, and dedication to the job (Montero-Marin et al., 2021). When practicing mindfulness, we actively pay attention to the present rather than dwelling on the past or anticipating the future (Psychology Today, 2023). For instance, some novice teachers I work with have committed to a 3-minute morning breathing exercise before heading to work in the morning and a few 1-minute "breathing breaks" throughout the school day. Neuroscience suggests that these types of routine mindfulness practices positively change the brain in areas that assist emotional regulation, empathy, stress management, learning, memory, and more. The research also suggests that simple and short mindfulness routines, even a 1- to 3-minute breathing break, can have lasting positive effects (Jennings, 2020; Tang et al., 2015).

In her book *Supporting Teacher Wellbeing*, Suzanne Allies (2021) offers guidance for teachers, mentors, and school leaders to promote whole-school well-being. Allies affirms that the self-care strategies of prioritizing physiological needs and mindfulness are especially fruitful for teachers to thrive. She also suggests that a schoolwide focus on well-being can promote teacher resilience and self-esteem. Mentors and school leaders can play an important role in supporting the well-being of their new teachers, which can lead teachers to thrive. For instance, one important way that mentors can boost new teacher well-being is by supporting classroom management—which is by far one of the biggest learning curves novices experience. In fact, Dicke and colleagues (2017) found that new teachers who felt supported and effective in classroom management had a healthier stress response than those who didn't. Hence, mentors can support mentees by offering robust classroom management guidance from classroom setup, effective procedures, direct modeling, coaching, encouragement, and feedback.

Finally, school leaders can make a significant impact on the collective well-being of their school personnel. Allies (2021) found that school leaders who prioritized an ethos of collective well-being had a positive school climate. Along with embracing well-being as a school-wide priority that can benefit staff and students alike, leaders can invest in the well-being and longevity of new teachers by ensuring they have the following:

- A less adverse class makeup than more experienced colleagues
- Consistent and direct support with challenging student behaviors
- At least one strong collegial relationship
- Same subject and/or grade-level mentors
- Opportunities to exercise their professional autonomy (Allies, 2021; Clark, 2012; De Clerq et al., 2022; Dicke et al., 2017; McLean et al., 2020)

SUPPORTING PRESERVICE AND EARLY CAREER TEACHERS: WELL-BEING HABITS

Over the last decade, personal well-being and self-care have gained considerable momentum in mainstream culture. This momentum has trickled down into several professions including health care, social work, and teaching (i.e., Allies, 2021; Boogren, 2018; Jennings, 2020; Montero-Marin et al., 2021; Zolkoski & Lewis-Chiu, 2019). However, in some cases, self-care has been commodified (Lieberman, 2018) and interpreted as limited and often pricey experiences such as spa days, yoga retreats, expensive vacations, and so on. While these experiences are indeed lovely, they are not accessible to everyone (especially on a teacher's salary!), and they do not promote healthy *habits*. Thoughtful habits and routines have a much more significant impact on well-being (Clear, 2018; Langshur & Klemp, 2016) than commercialized and costly experiences. Therefore, this section aims to share tools that novice teachers have found helpful as they work to establish sustainable self-care practices amid the inevitable time crunch and the emotional roller coaster that learning to teach engenders.

Given the busyness of a teacher's life, I've found that making small habit changes is most viable. Small changes support sustainable habit change (Clear, 2018) and feel less overwhelming to busy early career teachers. A favorite resource I draw from is Tina Boogren's *Take Time for You: Self-Care Action Plans for Educators* (2018). Based on positive psychology, this practical book equips teachers with surveys, action plans, and tools to improve their well-being. I use these resources and other well-being-oriented resources to impart the following tools to the novice teachers I support.

A Well-Being Conscious Meeting Routine

In all my workshops to support teachers thriving, I embed three important well-being routines into our agendas. I want our time together not to feel like yet another thing on a teacher's endless to-do list but instead, an opportunity for self- and collective care. I am candid with participants as to why these routines support our well-being:

1. **Mindfulness:** Given the benefits of just a few minutes of a mindfulness habit, we begin each session with a short, guided meditation, breathing, or other centering exercise to unwind from a busy day of teaching and to get grounded. I ask interested participants to sign up to facilitate these 5-minute sessions, and I am always impressed with what they bring (see Appendix A). For instance, one participant facilitated a mindfulness drawing exercise where we drew lines that followed our breath. Not only did this help relax and center the group, but we also had fun comparing our images.
2. **Connection:** Humans are social beings—belonging and connection are significant human needs (Maslow, 1943, 1972). However, being the only student teacher or new hire, or even one of a few, can feel lonely. Novice teachers need supportive relationships with peers, mentors, and people outside of their professional life to thrive. Therefore, I prioritize creating a community among my early career participants. I encourage them to connect beyond our time together, and many do. I establish group connection through a routine check-in immediately following the mindfulness exercise and lots of paired and small group dialogue about

the workshop's topics. A volunteer facilitates the check-in and offers a prompt related to our workshop topic (Appendix A). For instance, one member brought a teacher self-care bingo card that offered a playful means for small groups to identify ways they have or could attend to their well-being.

3. **Reflection:** Many teacher preparation programs encourage and assign reflection activities—reflecting on observations of experienced teachers, their emerging teacher identity, dispositions, a lesson they delivered, a challenging encounter with a student, and more (LaBelle & Belknap, 2016; Ryken & Hamel, 2016; Valtierra & Siegel, 2022). Teaching is not a perfect science. It is highly contextual and requires consistent trial and error. Therefore, teacher reflection is necessary to remaining true to our values. Teacher reflection promotes self-assessment of what worked, what didn't, and why. However, while most novices learn that reflection is essential, once in the classroom full time, the busyness of doing the work can make this practice easily fall by the wayside. Therefore, I ensure that workshops allow plenty of time for small group and personal reflection (Appendix A).

I also try to incorporate these routines into my teacher preparation coursework. While we don't typically take the time to engage in structured mindfulness or reflective journaling every class session, I do weave in regular opportunities for peer-to-peer connection around course materials and times for the other practices on a routine basis. In my context, wherein teacher candidates meet daily for coursework, I usually begin each Monday with mindfulness, check-ins to encourage connection, and setting intentions for the week ahead. Then, as the week unfolds, I block out deliberate time for connecting via paired and small group dialogue on course materials, time for personal journaling, and other reflection exercises.

Understanding Teachers' Hierarchy of Needs

Many educational psychology courses cover Maslow's hierarchy of needs (1943, 1972) to help teachers understand children's and adolescents' needs and behaviors. However, in her book *Take Time for*

Figure 5.1. Maslow's Hierarchy of Needs From the Lens of a Teacher

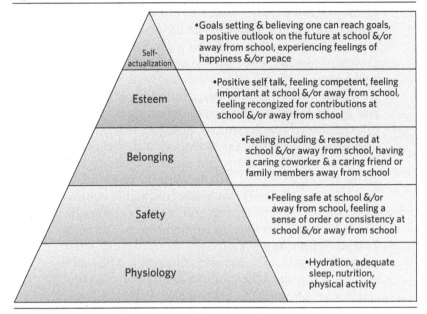

Note. Adapted from Maslow (1943, 1972) and Boogren (2018).

You, Tina Boogren (2018) encourages teachers to recognize and attend to their personal and professional hierarchy of needs. Adapted from Boogren, I've found reviewing Maslow's hierarchy from the lens of novice teacher well-being is validating and practical. I typically display the information in Figure 5.1 on a slide and/or distribute it as a handout. I like to talk through each need, starting at the bottom, the examples on the right, and invite participants to brainstorm tangible related experiences and possibilities. Our brainstorms typically include examples of habits to meet a particular need and firsthand accounts of when needs are not prioritized.

Needs-Based Well-Being Habit Changes

Next, I walk participants through the exercise that follows in Figure 5.2.

Checking In for Personal Well-Being

Boogren (2018) encourages teachers to develop a self–check-in habit, which is another form of mindfulness. Given the busyness

Figure 5.2. Teacher Well-Being: One Step at a Time

1. **Identify Your Needs:** Examine the descriptions on the right-hand side and starting from the bottom up (our most basic needs). Ask yourself:
   - Am I meeting my **physiological** needs?
     - » For example: Am I hydrated? Am I getting enough sleep most nights? Am I eating a nutritious diet most days? Am I moving my body most days? Am I proactively preparing to meet my physiological needs at school?
   - Do I feel **safe** and secure?
     - » For example: Do I feel safe at school? Do I feel a sense of order? Do I feel a sense of consistency? Is my classroom organized? Are my work expectations clear and consistent?
   - Do I feel **accepted** and have a sense of belonging?
     - » For example: Do I have positive colleagues I can collaborate with? Do I have at least one colleague who cares about my well-being? Do I feel accepted by my colleagues and administration? Do I feel I belong to a team?
   - Do I feel **confident** and respected?
     - » For example: Do I talk to myself like I would a person I love and respect? Do I recognize and celebrate my accomplishments, even the small wins? Do I feel like a respected member of my department, grade level, and/or school?
   - Am I reaching my full **potential**?
     - » For example: Do I set realistic goals that I believe I can accomplish? Do I have a positive outlook? Am I happy at school? Am I at peace?

2. **Start Small:** Identify the "lowest-hanging fruit" or most fundamental area of need on the hierarchy that could use attention.
   - Turn and talk to a peer about this need and a small related **habit** you can start tomorrow. For example:
     - » *"Starting tomorrow, I will bring a large water bottle and commit to sipping it throughout the day to feel hydrated,"* or
     - » *"Starting tomorrow, I am going to spend 15 minutes each morning organizing my classroom so that I feel a sense of order,"* or
     - » *"Starting tomorrow, I will schedule a weekly lunch date with one coworker to take a break and build relationships."*

3. **Write It Down:** Record your habit somewhere to remind yourself—on a Post-it Note, your digital calendar, a journal, and so on.
   - Keep track of your progress and be prepared to report back to us on your progress next week. Remember, progress, not perfection is key!

4. **Repeat:** Once your habit becomes automatic, repeat the process and find a tangible new habit to support your well-being!

Note. Adapted from Boogren (2018) and Maslow (1943, 1972).

of teaching, it's easy to be on autopilot and forget to recognize our feelings and needs. Hence, I've found it helpful to encourage this habit using the prompts in Figure 5.3. I typically distribute these prompts to participants and allow them time to complete it, followed by opportunity for willing participants to share with the wider group.

When our teachers feel cared for by their colleagues, mentors, and leadership and have the skills and agency to care for themselves, they are more likely to thrive. There is no doubt that early career teaching is a stressful time, and attending to personal well-being can help promising novices cope. Their state of mind also positively affects their students and the overall classroom environment. As Lexie, a 3rd-year elementary teacher, wisely recognized, "I tell myself that my students engage with my energy. That reminds me either to eat or feed my inner self. I cannot engage and connect with my students with disarray on the inside."

Figure 5.3. Checking-In Commitment for Teacher Well-Being

I will commit to recognizing how I feel at least_____ (3, 5, etc.) times per day. To stick to this commitment, I will_____.

(Examples: *set a phone reminder, include reminders in my lesson plan book, enlist an accountability buddy, habit bundle, etc.*)

At each check-in, I will get curious about my hierarchy of needs. I will ask myself, at this moment:

- Are my physiological needs met?
- Do I feel safe?
- Do I feel I belong?
- Do I feel confident?
- Do I feel optimistic?

I will notice how I feel, record it somewhere, and thank myself for tuning in. Self-awareness is powerful!

At the end of the week, I will identify patterns from my routine check-ins, celebrate the positives, and identify a commitment for next week. I am dedicated to progress, not perfection!

My well-being commitment for next week is to_____
_____. I will do this by_____.

Note. Adapted from Boogren (2018).

Figure 5.4. Chapter 5 Suggestions on How to Incorporate These Tools

Teacher Educators:
- Be transparent with teacher candidates about the well-being challenges many new teachers are prone to. Take time to proactively emphasize the importance of attending to personal well-being to thrive.
- Incorporate these tools into relevant coursework and/or workshops.
- Invite well-being experts to lead workshops on nutrition, mindfulness, and other practices. Invite more experienced teachers to share their well-being habits and why they are important.
- Include deliberate coursework on classroom management with a specific emphasis on identifying and managing challenging student behaviors.
- Include training on restorative practices, trauma-sensitive practices, and emotional regulation. The more equipped new teachers are to navigate these challenges, the more confident they will be.

Mentors:
- Routinely check in with your mentees using the hierarchy-of-needs prompts discussed above. Share ideas on how you attend to your well-being.
- Introduce new teachers to their colleagues. Help facilitate a sense of belonging.
- Point out novice teachers' strengths and growth toward their goals to help boost their confidence.
- Incorporate this workshop and suggested exercises into your teacher induction professional development sessions. This could be presented live, as virtual recorded materials, or in a hybrid fashion.
- Encourage a school climate of well-being. See Suzanne Allies *Supporting Teacher Wellbeing: A Practical Guide for Primary Teachers and School Leaders* (2021) and Elena Aguilar's *Onward: Cultivating Emotional Resilience in Educators* (2018) for proven and practical ideas.

New Teachers:
- Alone, or ideally with other novices, complete exercises I share to assess your current self-care routine and establish one or two new habits. Support each other and hold each other accountable! Check out Tina Boogren's *Take Time for You* (2018) for more resources and ideas.
- Find a creative way to bundle good habits that support your well-being. For instance, schedule a walk with a colleague during lunchtime. Then you are exercising and connecting at the same time! Or take turns prepping a simple yet healthy lunch for each other.
- The work of novice teaching can feel endless. Establish boundaries and a hard stopping point at the end of each day and workweek. Remind yourself that taking care of yourself is how you can replenish to care for your students. Invest in you to thrive!

INSIGHTS FROM PRESERVICE
AND EARLY CAREER TEACHERS

Over the years, I have found that often the most novice teachers who have participated in the exercises I describe above—student teachers and 1st-year teachers—were less attuned to their basic physiological needs. Like Anna, whom we met at the beginning of this chapter, carving out time for nutrition, let alone adequate exercise, felt like a stretch. Therefore, the well-being practices inspired them to commit to making these needs a priority. In contrast, most of the more experienced 2nd- or 3rd-year teachers had developed systems to support their more fundamental needs. As a result, they were ready to commit to their sense of safety, belonging, esteem, and/or self-actualization needs.

Starting Small

Most of the preservice and 1st-year teachers who participated in the self-care strategies detailed above recognized that their physiological needs had fallen by the wayside. Hence, these areas were a good place to commit to a small self-care habit. With these participants and other early career teachers I have worked with over the years, the need for hydration is a common trend. While this may sound simple, it's hard to drink enough water as a teacher. Students are in our classrooms for most of the day and can't be left unattended, and most passing periods are 5 minutes or less. Hence, it can feel impossible to take a bathroom break—making it challenging to stay hydrated. The struggle is real! Given this reality and the negative effect dehydration has on well-being, several new teachers committed to ensuring they are adequately hydrated and "finding a way to solve the bathroom conundrum" as a necessary initial well-being commitment. A few days after a well-being workshop session, student teacher Catherine emailed me this:

> Tina, thank you for reminding me to stay hydrated at school! It seems like common sense, but I've let it slip because I was too shy to brainstorm with [cooperating teacher] how to sneak in a bathroom break. It turns out we both needed to drink more water, so we've come up with a plan, and I already feel tons better throughout the day. Sometimes it's the little things!

Similarly, several of the newest teachers found the session a good reminder as to why getting adequate sleep, exercise, and healthy food is essential to supporting their well-being.

Building Up

Several of my 2nd- and 3rd-year teacher participants had established routines to meet their physiological needs at school. Others commented that they learned quickly that organizing their classroom environment contributed to their sense of safety. Layla reflected:

> My room was such a disaster my first year. I'd get to school and feel so overwhelmed by it and just avoid it. This made my teaching super disorganized and trickled down to the kids. Seriously, it was chaos. . . . So, when I finally asked [spouse] to help me organize, we took a whole weekend before this year started and cleaned things up. I can't tell you how much better I feel now in my classroom . . . and since then, I've worked to maintain it . . . and now that I think about it, it's related to giving the kids and me a sense of safety. I feel so much more calm and focused!

Several 2nd- and 3rd-year teacher participants were ready to commit to their sense of belonging, self-esteem, and/or optimism. Moreover, the teachers navigating a toxic school climate were reminded that rather than abandoning teaching altogether, they could seek a healthier school environment that would bolster their sense of belonging and well-being. For instance, Mike committed to his feelings of belonging by pushing himself to apply to open positions, recognizing that "I need to find a community and space that I feel comfortable in and that allows me to be me." Finally, Aubrey recognized that by surrounding herself with positive colleagues, she could improve her sense of self-esteem, belonging, and optimism:

> I want to commit to boosting self-esteem by surrounding myself with people who have positive outlooks on school and life in general. The people you spend your time with influence your self-esteem, and I think I have found myself as a vent for one particular staff member who has a very negative and pessimistic outlook on school and our teachers/students. In the same vein, there are so many people at our school who have the complete opposite outlook on school, and it boosts your passion and

esteem when you work with them. I want to start spending my time/ conversations more intentionally with staff who boost my self-esteem.

CONCLUSION: WELL-BEING AS HUMANIZATION

The central tenet of my conception of humanistic teacher development is valuing teachers as whole human beings. We must prioritize the needs of the "whole teacher," who is an emotional, intellectual, physical, mental, cultural, racialized, gendered, and spiritual being. I believe that the tools I impart in this chapter are a step in the right direction. New teachers need to be reminded that caring for themselves is vital to their capacity to thrive. Not only does teacher self-care support their general well-being, but it also supports their capacity to stay grounded in their purpose. Early career teachers who are deliberate about their well-being are more likely to have the capacity to prioritize teaching in ways that align with their values. Moreover, teaching for equity, and the school-level changes often required to do so, necessitates emotional bandwidth. In fact, mindfulness practices are found to support our ability to cope with and heal from the traumas that racism and other forms of oppression engender (Menakem, 2017). As such, self-care increases novices' resilience to the many stressors that come with early career teaching. Ultimately, teachers who prioritize their well-being are enacting their agency, supporting their resilience, and sustaining their purpose.

However, it is easy to let personal needs slip through the cracks when taking on the complex nature of learning to teach. Hence, novice teachers benefit from tangible tools they can incorporate into their busy schedules. And early career teachers need mentors who encourage them to take care of themselves and model their own self-care behaviors. Ultimately, when teachers are at their best, they are more equipped to support the well-being and success of their beloved students!

CHAPTER 6

Humanistic Teacher Development
Building Personalized Plans to Thrive

My mission in life is not merely to survive but to thrive; and to do so with some passion, some compassion, some humor, and some style.

—Maya Angelou

CHAPTER 6 GOALS

1. For readers to gain an overview of current literature on goal setting and habit building to support early career teachers to thrive
2. To provide readers with tools designed to help novice teachers author their personalized plans to thrive
3. To share one teacher's personalized plan that resulted from the exercises I detail

---

JORDAN DESIGNS A PLAN TO FLOURISH

Jordan, a first-generation college student, was highly engaged in youth organizing during his undergraduate degree. For instance, throughout his junior year, he participated in a program where he and his peers coached local high school students to identify problems in their community and organize for solution-oriented change. Inspired by these experiences, on entering an MAT program as an elementary teacher candidate, Jordan was motivated to find ways to involve his future students in the local community. His ultimate why for teaching was to "develop empathetic students who believe in themselves and their power to create change."

Jordan began his first position as a half-time 5th-grade teacher during the 2020–2021 school year. Most public schools were online,

93

hybrid, or adhering to another model due to the COVID-19 pandemic. Given the challenges of 1st-year teaching during a pandemic, Jordan decided to ease into his teaching career by accepting the part-time position his first year. This position led to a full-time 5th-grade offer for the following year. Initially a bit overwhelmed authoring a plan to thrive, Jordan participated in the exercises featured in this chapter. He developed a thoughtful personalized plan that gave him direction and confidence for his upcoming full-time position.

What follows are insights and exercises to help early career teachers like Jordan design individualized plans and routine habits to thrive. These exercises help sustain teachers' identities, proactively foster their resilience, and leverage their agency as equity-minded educators. Jordan's plan is featured as an inspiring example!

* * *

When teachers thrive, their students are more likely to thrive. It's contagious. Yet learning to teach can sometimes feel overwhelming. And, like Jordan initially felt, enacting a plan to thrive may feel like another thing on a new teacher's lengthy to-do list. Hence, proactively equipping novice teachers with tangible short-term and long-term well-being–oriented goals and benchmarks is important. If a teacher deliberately reflects and sets goals early on, they are likely to carry these ideas and skills with them throughout their career. Hence, the purpose of this chapter is to share tools for supporting novice teachers' well-being–oriented goals with concrete, identifiable habits and breaking goals down into manageable parts.

This chapter begins with an overview of the behaviors for which bestselling author James Clear (2018) coined the term "atomic habits," also commonly termed micro-commitments (Felkey et al., 2021). Taking cues from Clear's framework, I share insights on goal setting and building simple systems that can turn into ingrained habits. Equipping teachers with productive strategies that lead to well-being–oriented practices can help foster their self-efficacy (Bandura & Adams, 1977) and assist them in beginning their careers on a positive note.

Building off the topics in Chapters 2 through 5, readers will learn how to help new teachers set realistic goals around their ultimate why, their teacher development, managing tension, well-being, and more. Readers will learn how to establish associated habits and self-assess their progress. I provide activities designed to help early career

Humanistic Teacher Development

teachers tie together insights and practices from the topics explored in previous chapters. These scaffolded activities lead early career teachers to generate personalized plans that leverage their identity, resilience, and agency. Finally, I share Jordan's personalized plan, which exemplifies the power of proactively priming new educators to flourish.

SMALL HABITS LEAD TO BIG RESULTS

James Clear's 2018 *New York Times* bestseller *Atomic Habits: An Easy and Proven Way to Build Good Habits and Break Bad Ones* offers readers from all walks of life simple, evidence-based strategies to develop productive behaviors. Clear provides a straightforward and proven framework for breaking bad habits and starting new positive ones. He argues that small changes, or tiny habits, can make a big difference. In his words, "1% better every day ends with results that are almost 37% better after one year . . . habits are the compound interest of self-improvement" (p. 16).

According to Clear, the word *atomic* refers to a tiny quantity of a thing. It denotes a distinct irreducible element of a larger system and a vast power or energy source. *Habit* refers to a practice or routine executed consistently or an established reaction to a specific situation. While Clear uses the term "atomic habits" to describe his method of making small incremental changes over time, some psychological and economic researchers refer to these practices as micro-habits or micro-commitments (Felkey et al., 2021).

In my experience, Clear's strategies are highly adaptable and applicable when priming new teachers to thrive. His suggestions, in tandem with similar empirical research insights around goals, systems, and habits, are especially relevant for supporting novice teachers to create their personalized plans.

GOALS, SYSTEMS, AND HABITS

When goals are specific and challenging enough to motivate a person to pursue them, goal setting can improve performance (Locke et al., 1981). To support successful goal setting, in 1981, George Doran proposed the idea of SMART goals. Doran argued that setting Specific, Measurable, Attainable, Realistic, and Timely goals can help people clarify their thoughts, focus their energies, and effectively use their resources and time. The popular SMART framework is an established tool that can increase a person's chance of accomplishing their goals, including new teachers' goals around thriving in the profession.

In the case of supporting early career teachers to thrive, I have found that setting SMART goals is a great start. However, goals are not often achieved without committing to specific systems and related habits that support their attainment. As Clear (2018) argued, "goals are about the results you want to achieve. Systems are about the processes that lead to those results" (p. 21). As such, atomic habits, or micro-commitments, are the small habits that are part of a wider system or process designed to achieve one's goals. Complementing Clear's ideas, some authors delineate the importance of establishing outcome and smaller related "process goals" to achieve their intended result (Keith & Jagacinski, 2023).

Just as compound interest supports financial growth, the compound effect in habit building occurs when small changes over time lead to positive results. Over time, habits can multiply (Hardy, 2012). Moreover, research indicates that the more automated certain habits become, the more productivity is enhanced because your brain can focus on other tasks (Babauta, 2013; Clear, 2018; Housel, 2017). When we can prepare novice teachers to begin their careers with specific goals for thriving, related systems, and micro-commitments, the small habits they commit to can soon become an automatic part of their daily routine.

Clear (2018) writes that there are three levels of habit formation: outcome, process, and identity based. Outcome-based habits focus on *what* you want to achieve, process-based habits focus on *how* you will achieve your goals, and identity-based habits inspire *who you want to become*. Clear argues that the most effective way to establish habits is to focus not on what you want to achieve but on who you wish to become. Hence, drawing a parallel to priming early career teachers to flourish, what follows are a series of scaffolded exercises I have used to help teachers establish goals, benchmarks, and habits that proactively center their aspiration to become thriving educators. Inspired by Clear's proven framework, the following section features tools to support preservice and early career teachers in formulating personalized plans that will crystalize their professional identities and encourage resilience and agency.

SUPPORTING PRESERVICE AND EARLY CAREER TEACHERS: PERSONALIZED PLANS TO THRIVE

This book offers tools designed to promote novice teachers' identity, resilience, and agency in hopes that they thrive in the profession. To do this, I have found that developing personalized plans for thriving should be deliberate and focused. I slowly take participating teachers through the following exercises using a scaffolded series of independent assignments and one workshop gathering. The independent assignments allow participating teachers to carefully reflect and take their time establishing a plan that resonates with them. Then the workshop creates an opportunity for direct support and collaboration.

Building from their ultimate why discussed in Chapter 2, my process begins with supporting early career teachers to crystallize their teaching values, vision, and mission. Next, I guide them through an outcome–goal-setting exercise. Then they identify related process goals and benchmarks. Finally, we drill all the prior work down into daily micro-commitments. Each step of my process aims to ensure that teachers' personalized plans lead to tangible identity-based habits.

Uncovering Teacher Values

Before our first meeting, I like to send the assignment steps depicted in Figure 6.1 to participants and ask them to come to our meeting prepared to share and discuss their teacher values and drafted vision and mission statements.

It's important to acknowledge that drilling down to a few core values can be challenging. Yet having too many values can dilute our capacity to develop a focused plan. I often encourage teachers to categorize similar values and then determine the word that best represents the sentiment of those related ideas. As mentioned in previous chapters, I rely heavily on reflective journaling throughout the exercises shared in this book. Hence, using their journals to uncover their teacher values works well for the educators I support. However, teacher values can also be uncovered by asking participants to review a list of core values and choose the top few that best represent them. There are many lists of core values easily accessible online and in the literature. Some of my favorites include a list of core values in Brené Brown's book *Dare to Lead* (2018), James Clear's list on his website (https://jamesclear.com

Figure 6.1. Identifying Your Teacher Values

Teacher Values: *Your individual beliefs that inform your professional behaviors.*

Step 1: Revisit your ultimate why for being a teacher.

Step 2: With your why in mind, read your Teach and Thrive journal entries and highlight words and phrases reflecting your teacher values.

Step 3: Make a list of all highlighted words and phrases.

Step 4: Sort the list by repeating and/or similar words or phrases.

Step 5: Count repeating and/or similar words or phrases.

Step 6: Determine the top three to four teacher values.

Note. Adapted from Valtierra & Siegel (2022).

/core-values), and a list by author Scott Jeffrey, which is also available on his website (https://scottjeffrey.com/core-values-list/).

Early Career Teacher Vision and Mission Statements

The teacher values serve as a catalyst for participants to develop their personal vision and mission statements. Their teacher values, early career vision, and mission statements help novice teachers clarify their professional identities, determine how to enact their why, and design a plan to thrive. I like to begin by ensuring that participants clearly understand the purpose of a vision and mission statement. Hence, I provide the information in Figure 6.2 as a handout.

Next, I prompt participants to take some time to journal using the prompts in Figure 6.3. The purpose of these prompts is to guide teachers to develop their vision and mission statements.

Finally, I ask participants to use the work above to help them draft their teaching vision and mission statements to share and refine in our meeting. I instruct them to make each statement one or two sentences maximum that they can easily remember and refer to on a routine basis. These statements should express the values they want to live and work by and help them feel inspired when they read them.

Designing Personal Plans to Thrive

I ask participants to come to our goal-setting workshop session prepared to share their values, vision, and mission statements. I typically put participants in small groups of two or more to share and offer

Humanistic Teacher Development 99

Figure 6.2. Teacher Vision and Mission Statements

The **teacher vision statement** describes what you want to achieve in the future. It inspires your optimal thriving teacher self, aligns with your teacher values, and connects to your purpose. Your early career vision statement should reflect the teacher you hope to become 5 years from now.

The **mission statement** describes what you want to achieve now and how you will incrementally work toward your vision statement. This statement strategically ties your present to your future.

Figure 6.3. Uncovering Your Early Career Vision and Mission Statement Journal Prompts

1. What personal qualities do you want to shine through in your classroom? Your school and community?
2. How can you demonstrate these personal qualities in your teaching?
3. How will you express your teacher values in the classroom? With colleagues? Families? Community members?
4. Visualize yourself 5 years from now:
   - Imagine yourself as a thriving professional teacher. Imagine that everything is exactly as you hope it will be: your classroom environment, your curriculum and lessons, your relationships with students, colleagues, families, and more. Write, take notes, and/or draw what you see.
   - Keep imagining your future thriving teacher self, and be as specific as you can be. Where are you? Who are your students? What are you doing? What are they doing? How does it feel? Write, take notes, and/or draw what you see.
   - Keep imagining your future thriving teacher self. What impact are you having on your students? Colleagues? School? Local community? The teaching profession?

Note. Adapted from LiquidPlanner.com (2022).

one another feedback on their statements. Next, we share our insights from hearing one another's statements and spend a little time workshopping and refining statements. From there, I give a brief lecture on goal setting, inspired by James Clear's (2018) framework. I discuss the information in Figure 6.4 projected as a slide and provided as a handout for future reference.

Next, with the above terminology in mind, I lead participants through a series of goal-setting exercises for each teacher wellbeing topic explored in this book. We begin by setting big-picture,

Figure 6.4. Outcome, Process and Micro-Commitments to Thrive

Personalized Plans to Thrive: Outcome, Process, and Micro-Commitments

Outcome Goal: *What* you want to achieve as an early career teacher.
Process Goal: The systems you will commit to. *How* you will achieve your outcomes.
Identity Goal: *Who* you want to be in your role as a teacher. Should connect directly to your outcome and process goals.
Micro-commitment: The daily small **habits** you will commit to achieve your goals.

The power of micro-commitments: *"1% better every day ends with results that are almost 37% better after one year . . . habits are the compound interest of self-improvement."*
(James Clear, 2018, p. 16).

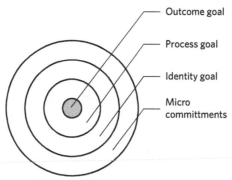

Benchmark: How you will measure your progress on a routine basis.

outcome-oriented SMART goals and then breaking them into annual benchmarks and relevant process goals. Finally, we drill down the process goals into tangible daily micro-commitments. Over the years, I have learned that many participating teachers benefit from doing the following exercises with a thought partner. Hence, I usually pair teachers up to work side by side and invite them to dialogue as they work. Most participants I work with are familiar with SMART goals, but reviewing the acronym and purpose is a good reminder. As delineated below in Figure 6.5, I like to use an adapted *SMARRT* goals version for this exercise that adds an extra R for "Realistic" so that teachers are reminded to adopt small habits that are viable, rather than committing to lofty goals that may get derailed due to competing priorities.

Humanistic Teacher Development

Figure 6.5. Goal Setting to Thrive Template

5-Year Goals	Outcome #1 Sustaining Purpose	Outcome #2 Teacher Development	Outcome #3 Tension/ Conflict	Outcome #4 Well- Being	Outcome #5 Other (Optional)
Instructions: For each teacher focus area, use your values, vision, and mission to complete the worksheet below to draft one SMARRT Outcome Goal you plan to reach in 5 years.					
Specific					
Measurable					
Attainable					
Relevant					
Realistic					
Timely (5 years)					

Once participants have drafted their SMARRT goals, we often debrief the process and offer one another encouragement and feedback. Next, we move to the process goal and benchmark exercise shown in Figure 6.6.

Finally, once participants have completed the exercise above, we move to the micro-commitment worksheet shown in Figure 6.7. I've found it's often helpful to provide participants with a few examples, such as the one provided in the section that follows from Jordan's plan.

When novice teachers can drill down to specific identity-based micro-commitments that keep them focused on the thrival-oriented topics unpacked in this book, they can proactively practice the behaviors they identified. This can help set them up to enter the profession prepared to flourish.

Figure 6.6. Process Goals and Benchmarks.

Instructions: Copy and paste each SMARRT goal into the top box of the worksheet, and then backward map one annual *benchmark* and *process goal* for years 1–4.

	Outcome #1 Sustaining Purpose	Outcome #2 Teacher Development	Outcome #3 Tension/ Conflict	Outcome #4 Wellbeing	Outcome #5 Other (Optional)
Year 5: **Outcome Goal**					
(SMARRT goal from above)					
Year 4: Benchmark					
Year 4: Process Goal					
Year 3: Benchmark					
Year 3: Process Goal					
Year 2: Benchmark					
Year 2: Process Goal					
Year 1: Benchmark					
Year 1: Process Goal					

Figure 6.7. Teacher Micro-Commitments to Thrive

Instructions: For year 1, copy and paste the benchmark and process goal. Then determine a daily micro-commitment that will help you achieve your goal.

	Outcome #1 Sustaining Purpose	Outcome #2 Teacher Development	Outcome #3 Tension/ Conflict	Outcome #4 Well-Being	Outcome #5 Other (Optional)
Year 1 Benchmark and Process Goal					
Daily Micro-Commitment					

Figure 6.8. Chapter 6 Suggestions on How to Incorporate These Tools

Teacher Educators:
- Incorporate the process I share into relevant coursework and/or workshops.
- Include a program-long virtual teacher course that ends with teacher candidates authoring their personalized plans to thrive.
- Be deliberate about illustrating the parallel between teacher candidates daily habits for thriving and supporting their students.

Mentors:
- Incorporate the exercises and resulting personalized plan to thrive into your teacher induction professional development sessions. This could be presented live, as virtual recorded materials, or in a hybrid fashion.
- Then check in regularly around the plan and your mentees' micro-commitments. Help them problem solve and revise their plan as needed.

New Teachers:
- Use the prompts and exercises I share to independently, or with a group of early career teachers, develop your personalized plans to thrive.
- Find a creative and inspiring way to display and remind yourself daily of your micro-commitments. Early career teachers I know often set alarms on their phone to prompt their new habits.
- Share your micro-commitments, process, and outcome goals with your mentors and peers. Ask for their support in reaching these important goals.

JORDAN'S PERSONALIZED PLAN TO THRIVE

Jordan, whom we met at the opening of this chapter, participated in the exercises described above. Foremost, after reviewing his ultimate why, Jordan narrowed his teacher values to *Community, Equity, Empathy*, and *Growth-Mindset*. His vision and mission were as follows:

> My vision is to be a passionate 5th-grade teacher who embodies my empathetic nature to promote an empowering and equitable classroom community. I aim to develop a growth mindset in all my students as we engage directly in the local community to apply curriculum for the greater good. My mission is to build empathy in my students to create a strong and equitable learning community.

Jordan's outcome goals for each topic are shown in Figure 6.9.

Jordan's SMARRT goals then led to the benchmark and process goals for Sustaining Purpose depicted in Figure 6.10.

Figure 6.9. Jordan's Goal Setting to Thrive

Instructions: For each focus area, use your vision and mission to complete the worksheet below to draft one SMARRT Outcome Goal you plan to reach in 5 years.					
5-Year Goals	Outcome #1 Sustaining Purpose	Outcome #2 Teacher Development	Outcome #3 Tension/ Conflict	Outcome #4 Well-Being	Outcome #5 Other (Optional)
Specific Measurable Attainable Relevant Realistic Timely (5 years)	Five school years from now, I will end most workweeks (80–90%) feeling I have upheld and grown my passion for working with and showing empathy for diverse upper-elementary students.	Five school years from now, I will have the confidence and expertise to implement community-based learning in at least two core subject areas: social studies and reading.	Five school years from now, I will be able to productively address conflict and tension with my students, their families, my colleagues, and the administration at least 75% of the time.	Five school years from now, I will not bring work home at night, on weekends, or during breaks 100% of the time.	Five years from now, I will lead professional development and mentor colleagues in community-based learning. I will take on this leadership role in my school and at least one other local school.

Figure 6.10. Jordan's Benchmark and Process for Outcome Goal #1

Instructions: Copy and paste each SMARRT goal into the top of the worksheet, and then backward map one annual *benchmark assessment* and *process goal* for years 1–4.	
Year 5: Outcome Goal (SMARRT goal from above)	Five school years from now, I will end most workweeks (80–90%) feeling I have upheld and grown my passion for working with and showing empathy for diverse upper-elementary students.
Year 4: Benchmark	By the end of the school year, I will have implemented at least two next steps from student suggestions and feel my vision is realized at least 70% of the time.
Year 4: Process Goal	At least three times during the school year (September, December, and March), I will ask my students, via conversation and a short questionnaire, what I am doing well and what I can do differently to realize my vision. I will collaborate with my students to act on at least two of their suggestions.
Year 3: Benchmark	By the end of the school year, I will have implemented at least two next steps discovered through conversations with mentors and colleagues. I will feel closer to reaching my vision.
Year 3: Process Goal	During winter break and the summer before the school year, I will spend some time making a list of steps to reach my vision. I will collaborate with mentors or colleagues to find two action steps to implement in my classroom.
Year 2: Benchmark	By the end of the school year, I will have implemented at least three next steps from the summer list made in my process goal. I will feel like my classroom reflects my mission.
Year 2: Process Goal	I will spend some time in the summer before the school year making a list of things that get in the way of my mission. I will ask my mentor for feedback on my strengths and the next steps to implement to realize my mission.
Year 1: Benchmark	By the end of the year, I will have an automatic routine of reciting and reflecting on my teacher's values, vision, and mission at the start of each morning.
Year 1: Process Goal	I will display my teacher's values, vision, and mission somewhere prominent I can see on my desk.

Figure 6.11. Jordan's Micro-Commitment to Thrive Outcome #1

Instructions: For each Year 1 process goal, copy and paste the benchmark and process goal. Then determine a daily micro-commitment that will help you achieve your goal.	
Year 1 Benchmark and Process Goal	B: By the end of the year, I will have an automatic daily habit of reciting and reflecting on my teacher values, vision, and mission at the start of each morning. P: I will display my teacher values, vision, and mission somewhere prominent I can see on my desk.
Daily Micro-Commitment	When I get to work each morning, I will set an alarm on my phone to remember to read and think of at least one way to realize my teacher values, vision, and mission before I start my day.

Finally, Jordan developed the micro-commitment shown in Figure 6.11 to reach his goal during his first year in his new position.

Through the processes outlined above, Jordan and other participating early career teachers developed thoughtful and viable identity-based plans to thrive. In his final reflection on the personalized planning process, Jordan wrote:

> When we first started these activities, I was overwhelmed. In teaching, there's just so much to do, and I worried this was going to be way too much for me. But by breaking my goals down into small habits, I feel pretty confident I can make these habits stick and hopefully be the 5th-grade teacher I dream of.

Similarly, Jordan's peers who participated in the process most frequently reflected that their plans gave them "hope," "inspiration," "direction," and as Delia noted, helped "frame becoming a thriving, well-balanced teacher as something doable . . . a lot of work and commitment, but within reach!"

CONCLUSION: STRATEGIZING TO THRIVE

Learning to teach is demanding and challenging. Typically, education programs prepare novices for the technical aspects of the profession: lesson planning, assessment, grading, classroom management, aligning instruction with standards, and more. While these skills are vital to student academic success, I argue that novice teachers also require proactive and explicit support to flourish—which ultimately benefits their students. We must prepare and nourish novice teachers to thrive so that they can realize their professional goals and sustain their passion for the profession. Without encouragement to explicitly plan to thrive, early career teachers are at risk of burnout and prematurely exiting the profession. Yet with support, they are set up to become the teacher they aspire to be.

By uncovering their core values and developing their teaching mission and vision, new teachers can discover tangible ways to make their emerging teacher identity come to life in the classroom. Moreover, by carefully connecting their mission and vision to a 5-year plan, they can break down their aspirations into smaller, realistic steps. Finally, daily micro-commitments make it more likely that novice teachers will have the time and space to realize their aspirations. Personalized plans to thrive can help novices leverage their unique professional identity, resilience, and agency to prosper as educators. This, in turn, will increase the likelihood that their beloved students prosper as well!

CONCLUSION

A Call to Support Teachers to Thrive

A good teacher is like a candle—it consumes itself to light the way for others.

—Mustafa Kemal Atatürk

Teachers are the backbone of society. An amazing teacher can profoundly influence a young person's life. When teachers thrive, they can harness radical hope, creativity, joy, intellectual curiosity, and more. Yet too many new teachers experience extreme burnout, disillusionment, and/or demoralization and prematurely give up on the profession. This, in turn, deprives youth, schools, and education systems of the promise and potential these aspiring change makers could impart.

Teacher burnout and attrition disproportionately affect our most marginalized schools, the youth, and communities they serve (NCES, 2019; Nguyen & Springer, 2021; Papay et al., 2015; Ulferts, 2016). Furthermore, BIPOC, disabled, and LGBTQ+ teachers are more susceptible to turnover than their more privileged colleagues (Mahatmya et al., 2021; Rios & Longoria, 2021). These disproportionalities recycle systemic inequities, rob marginalized youth of valuable role models, and deprive the profession of passionate change agents. Moreover, critically conscious teachers of all backgrounds who are committed to culturally sustaining pedagogy cannot adequately actualize these approaches in unstable environments where teacher churn is endemic. It is only when motivated and committed teachers of all walks of life are equipped to flourish that they can fully deliver CSP.

I dream of an education system designed for all teachers to flourish. Rather than leaving their ability to thrive to chance, I hope for a system that prioritizes and invests in preparing new teachers to succeed from the get-go. I hope we move toward a cohesive and collaborative system that unites stakeholders in education, including teacher preparation, early career induction, mentoring, professional development programs, school and district leaders, policymakers, and classroom teachers. If we come together to prime our newest teachers to thrive, their students will benefit from committed, high-quality, passionate educators. Successful teachers, in turn, can engender more equitable, inclusive, and inspiring societies. *Preparing Early Career Teachers to Thrive* is for fellow educators who share my aspirations.

The ideas that guide this book are informed by merging theories of humanistic learning, multicultural education, and strategies I have field tested over the years to proactively support novice teachers to thrive. While most teacher preparation and early career induction curricula center on the methodological aspects of teaching, I argue that we need to add a humanizing component to prime novice teachers to succeed. As such, my conceptual framework of humanistic teacher development argues that to prepare early career teachers to flourish, stakeholders should:

- Honor the fact that teachers are full human beings and thus attend to the "whole teacher," who is an emotional, intellectual, physical, mental, cultural, racialized, gendered, and spiritual person;
- Facilitate opportunities for regular self-evaluation for new teachers to track their progress, set incremental goals, embrace praxis; and
- Empower new teachers to choose how they achieve their professional responsibilities by considering their identities, beliefs, values, strengths, goals, and school community context.

To do this, stakeholders should attend to the personal and conditional factors known to influence a teacher's ability to thrive. A teacher's professional identity, resilience, and agency are valuable individual qualities that novices can cultivate. These three attributes operate interchangeably to support teacher well-being. Concurrently, several conditional factors contribute to a new teacher's success, including targeted mentorship, an affirming school environment, administrator support, and strong collegial relationships. Combined, proactive attention to the personal and contextual factors that advance teachers' success can potentially reverse the early career teacher turnover crisis and promote equity by keeping critically conscious novices in the field.

Using the resources and practices I impart throughout this book is an important step toward establishing early career teachers' capacities to succeed. In tandem with the tools and insights I offer, we need to collectively advocate for structural change in our schooling systems. What we are doing right now is not working. Too many promising new teachers are calling it quits before they have had the opportunity to realize their potential. We cannot reverse this alarming trend without fighting for the school conditions and policies needed for all teachers to thrive. While this book offers readers in a variety of contexts and roles actionable steps to support early career teachers, we also must push policymakers at all levels to ensure our education systems are equipped to provide educators with the resources, professional autonomy, and school environments that promote well-being. Ultimately, if we care about education systems, schools, and the welfare of youth, we need to cherish teachers. Thriving teachers are our ticket to fulfilling the promise of education.

The topics featured in this book were garnered from the literature along with several years of collecting novice teachers' stories, ideas, concerns, and priorities. However, given that the specific needs of early career teachers in varied settings may differ from the participants featured in this book, I encourage readers to modify the tools I share as you see fit. For instance, you might pick and choose specific exercises that resonate with you and the early career teachers in your community. Or you might come up with another topic that is important to the teachers in your community and use the meeting agenda template to structure your time together (Appendix A). Drop me a line and share your adaptations and ideas! Together we can foster change. Just as the African proverb argues that "it takes a village to raise a child," it takes a village to prepare, retain, and sustain our next generation of promising teachers. We are in this together.

APPENDIX

TTLC Workshop Agenda Template

1. Centering/Mindfulness (3–5 min)
Purpose: to practice well-being tools to support our resilience.
Facilitator(s):

2. Check-In (15–20 min)
Purpose: to build community.
Facilitator(s):

3. Teach and Thrive Topic (45 min)
Purpose: to understand important topics that can build our
resilience, agency, and teacher identities.
Facilitator(s):
Topic:

114   Preparing Early Career Teachers to Thrive

4. Written Self-Reflection (10–15 min)
  Purpose: to facilitate praxis (reflection and action) to help us explore
    our teacher identities.
  Facilitator(s):

5. Housekeeping/Announcements

References

Aguilar, E. (2018). *Onward: Cultivating emotional resilience in educators.* Jossey-Bass.

Ainsworth, S., & Oldfield, J. (2019). Quantifying teacher resilience: Context matters. *Teaching and Teacher Education, 82,* 117–128. https://doi.org/10.1016/j.tate.2019.03.012

Alifah, P. (2018). Multicultural education and humanism theory as an effort to improve the social sensibility of primary school students. *Varia Pendidikan, 30*(1), 73–78. https://journals.ums.ac.id/index.php/varidika/article/view/6547/0

Allen, J. (2000). Teaching about multicultural and diversity issues from an humanistic perspective. *American Education Research Association.* https://files.eric.ed.gov/fulltext/ED443791.pdf

Alliance for Excellent Education (AEE). (2014). *On the path to equity: Improving the effectiveness of beginning teachers.* 1–17. https://all4ed.org/publication/path-to-equity

Allies, S. (2021). *Supporting teacher wellbeing: A practical guide for primary teachers and school leaders.* Routledge.

Alsup, J. (2019). Teacher identity discourse as identity growth: Stories of authority and vulnerability. In P. Schutz, J. Y. Hong, & D. Cross Francis (Eds.), *Research on teacher identity: Mapping challenges and innovations* (pp. 13–23). Springer Nature.

Alvariñas-Villaverde, M., Domínguez-Alonso, J., Pumares-Lavandeira, L., & Portela-Pino, I. (2022). Initial motivations for choosing teaching as a career. *Frontiers in Psychology, 13.* https://doi.org/10.3389/fpsyg.2022.842557

American Psychiatric Association. (2013). *Diagnostic and statistical manual of mental disorders* (5th ed.). American Psychiatric Association, Arlington, VA. www.psych.org.

American Psychological Association (APA). (2023). *Well-being.* https://dictionary.apa.org/well-being

Anderson, D., Cameron-Standerford, A., Bergh, B., & Bohjanen, S. (2019). Teacher evaluation and its impact on wellbeing: Perceptions of Michigan teachers and administrators. *Education, 139*(3), 139–150. https://www

.ingentaconnect.com/content/prin/ed/2019/00000139/00000003/art00005

Anderson, L., & Olsen, B. (2006). Investigating early career urban teachers' perspectives on and experiences in professional development. *Journal of Teacher Education, 57*, 359–377. https://doi.org/10.1177/0022487106291565

Au, W. (2009). *Unequal by design: High-stakes testing and the standardization of inequality.* Routledge.

Au, W. (2017). When multicultural education is not enough. *Multicultural Perspectives, 19*(3), 147–150. https://doi.org/10.1080/15210960.2017.1331741

Austin, J. R., & Koerner, B. D. (2016, March). The role of teacher resilience in combating music teacher turnover at different career stages [Conference session]. *National Association for Music Education Music Research and Teacher Education National Conference*, Atlanta, GA, United States.

Babauta, L. (2013). *The power of habit investments.* https://zenhabits.net/bank/

Baliram, N., Koetje, K., & Huff, E. (2021). Virtual learning environments and a needs assessment of K–12 teachers. *AILACTE Journal, 18*, 27–53. https://ailacte.org/images/downloads/ailacte21_for_web_apr1.pdf

Ball, S. J. (2003). The teacher's soul and the terrors of performativity. *Journal of Education Policy, 18*(2), 215–228. https://doi.org/10.1080/0268093022000043065

Bandura, A., & Adams, N. E. (1977). Analysis of self-efficacy theory of behavioral change. *Cognitive Therapy and Research, 1*(4), 287–310. https://doi.org/10.1007/BF01663995

Banks, J. A. (1993). Multicultural education: Historical development, dimensions, and practice. *Review of Research in Education, 19*, 3–49.

Barkatsas, A., & Malone, J. (2005). A typology of mathematics teachers' beliefs about teaching and learning mathematics and instructional practices. *Mathematics Education Research Journal, 17*(2), 69–90. https://doi.org/10.1007/bf03217416

Beijaard, D. (2019). Teacher learning as identity learning: Models, practices, and topics. *Teachers and Teaching: Theory and Practice, 25*(1), 1–6. https://doi.org/10.1080/13540602.2019.1542871

Bieler, D., Holmes, S., & Wolfe, E. W. (2016). Patterns in the initial teaching assignments of secondary English teachers: Implications for teacher agency and retention. *The New Educator, 13*(1), 22–40. https://doi.org/10.1080/1547688x.2016.1144119

Biesta, G., Priestley, M., & Robinson, S. (2015). The role of beliefs in teacher agency. *Teachers and Teaching: Theory and Practice, 21*(6), 624–640. http://dx.doi.org/10.1080/13540602.2015.1044325

References

Bonilla-Silva, E. (2006). *Racism without racists: Color-blind racism and the persistence of racial inequality in the United States.* Rowman & Littlefield.

Boogren, T. (2018). *Take time for you: Self-care action plans for teachers.* Solution Tree.

Boogren, T. (2021). *Supporting beginning teachers: Tips for beginning teacher support to reduce teacher stress and burnout.* Marzano Research.

Bressman, S., Winter, J. S., & Efron, S. E. (2018). Next-generation mentoring: Supporting teachers beyond induction. *Teaching and Teacher Education, 73,* 162–170. https://doi.org/10.1016/j.tate.2018.04.003

Brown, B. (2018). *Dare to lead: Brave work, tough conversations, full hearts.* Random House.

Buchanan, J., Prescott, A., Schuck, S., Aubusson, P., Burke, P., & Louviere, J. (2013). Teacher retention and attrition: Views of early career teachers. *Australian Journal of Teacher Education, 38*(3), 112–129. https://doi.org/10.14221/ajte.2013v38n3.9

Cabrera, C. M. (2013). *Relationship of teachers' perceptions of organizational health and workplace bullying.* (Doctoral dissertation, Fairleigh Dickinson University). Proquest Dissertations Publishing.

Castro, A. J., Kelly, J., & Shih, M. (2010). Resilience strategies for new teachers in high-needs areas. *Teaching and Teacher Education, 26*(3), 622–629. https://doi.org/10.1016/j.tate.2009.09.010

Center for Applied Special Technology (CAST). (2022). *About universal design for learning.* https://www.cast.org/impact/universal-design-for-learning-udl

Chan, M-K., Sharkey, J. D., Lawrie, S. I., Arch, D. A. N., & Nylund-Gibson, K. (2021). Elementary school teacher well-being and supportive measures amid COVID-19: An exploratory study. *School Psychology, 36*(6), 533–545. https://doi.org/10.1037/spq0000441

Christensen, J. C., & Fessler, R. (1992). Teacher development as a career-long process. In R. Fessler & J. C. Christensen (Eds.), *The teacher career cycle: Understanding and guiding the professional development of teachers* (pp.–20). Allyn & Bacon.

Clark, S. K. (2012). The plight of the novice teacher. *The Clearing House: A Journal of Educational Strategies, Issues, and Ideas, 85*(5), 197–200. https://doi.org/10.1080/00098655.2012.689783

Clear, J. (2018). *Atomic habits: An easy and proven way to build good habits and break bad ones.* Avery.

Clear, J. (2023). *Core values list.* https://jamesclear.com/core-values

Cobb, D. J. (2022). Metaphorically drawing the transition into teaching: What early career teachers reveal about identity, resilience, and agency. *Teaching and Teacher Education, 110.* https://doi.org/10.1016/j.tate.2021.103598

Cohen, R. M. (2022, February 16). *As states build barriers to racial justice teaching, educators fight back.* Rethinking Schools. Retrieved February 2, 2023, from https://rethinkingschools.org/articles/as-states-build-barriers-to-racial-justice-teaching-educators-fight-back

Connelly, F. M., & Clandinin, D. J. (2004). *Narrative inquiry: Experience and story in qualitative research.* Jossey Bass.

Costello, M. B. (2016, November 28). *The Trump effect.* Southern Poverty Law Center. https://www.splcenter.org/sites/default/files/splc_the_trump_effect.pdf

Council for the Accreditation of Educator Preparation (CAEP). (2022). *2022 CAEP standards.* https://caepnet.org/standards/2022-itp/introduction

Coutler, S., & Lester, J. N. (2011). Finding and redefining the meaning of teaching: Exploring the experiences of mid-career teachers. *Journal of Curriculum and Instruction, 5*(2), 5–26. https://doi.org/10.3776/joci.2011.v5n2p5-26

Cowie, H., Naylor, P., Rivers, I., Smith, P. K., & Pereira, B. (2002). Measuring workplace bullying. *Aggression and Violent Behavior, 7*(1), 33–51. https://doi.org/10.1016/S1359-1789(00)00034-3

Crain, W. (2015). *Theories of development: Concepts and applications* (6th ed.). Routledge.

Cuban, L. (2010, April 20). *How long does it take to become a "good" teacher?* Word Press. https://larrycuban.wordpress.com/2010/04/20/how-long-does-it-take-to-become-a-good-teacher

Dantley, M. E. (2003). Critical spirituality: Enhancing transformative leadership through critical theory and African American prophetic spirituality. *International Journal of Leadership in Education: Theory and Practice, 6*(1), 3–17. https://www.tandfonline.com/doi/abs/10.1080/1360312022000069987

Darling-Hammond, L. (2000). Teacher quality and student achievement: A review of state policy evidence. *Education Policy Analysis Archives, 8*, 1. https://doi.org/10.14507/epaa.v8n1.2000

Darling-Hammond, L. (2010). *The flat world and education: How America's commitment to equity will determine our future.* Teachers College Press.

Daugherty, A. A. (2019). *Unstressed: How somatic awareness can transform your body's stress response and build emotional resilience.* New Harbinger.

Day, C. (2018). Professional identity matters: Agency, emotions, and resilience. In P. A. Schutz, J. Hong, & D. C. Francis (Eds.), *Research on teacher identity: Mapping challenges and innovations* (pp. 61–70). Springer.

De Clercq, M., Watt, H. M. G., & Richardson, P. W. (2022). Profiles of teachers' striving and wellbeing: Evolution and relations with context factors, retention, and professional engagement. *Journal of Educational Psychology, 114*(3), 637–655. https://doi.org/10.1037/edu0000702

References

119

Dell'Angelo, T. (2021). *Down the rabbit hole*: An ethnodrama to explore a fantastical first year of teaching. *Qualitative Inquiry, 27*(1), 77–84. https://doi.org/10.1177/1077800419879192

Diamond, J., & Spillane, J. (2004). High-stakes accountability in urban elementary schools: Challenging or reproducing inequality? *Teachers College Record, 106*(6), 1145–1176. https://doi.org/10.1111/j.1467-9620.2004.00375.x

Dicke, T., Stebner, F., Linninger, C., Kunter, M., & Leutner, D. (2017). A longitudinal study of teachers' occupational well-being: Applying the job demands-resource model. *Journal of Occupational Health Psychology, 23*(2), 262–277. http://dx.doi.org/10.1037/ocp0000070

Doran, G. T. (1981). There's a SMART way to write management's goals and objectives. *Journal of Management Review, 70*, 35–36. https://community.mis.temple.edu/mis0855002fall2015/files/2015/10/S.M.A.R.T-Way-Management-Review.pdf

Dos Santos, L. M. (2020). Becoming a pre-school and elementary school educator: How do male teachers describe their career decision and career development from the perspective of the social cognitive career approach and human resource management. *Journal of Education and e-Learning Research, 7*(2), 159–166. https://doi.org/10.20448/journal.509.2020.72.159.166

Duchesne, S., & McMaugh, A. (2015). *Educational psychology for learning and teaching*. Cengage Learning.

Dunn, A. H. (2018). Leaving a profession after it's left you: Teachers' public resignation letters as resistance amidst neoliberalism. *Teachers College Record, 120*(9), 1–34.

Endo, R. (2021). On holding various truths to (not) be self-evident: Leading during the dual pandemics of 2020 as a racialized body. *Cultural Studies ↔ Critical Methodologies, 21*(1), 116–121. https://doi.org/10.1177/1532708620960171

Epstein, J. (2018). *School, family, and community partnerships: Your handbook for action*. Corwin.

Ericsson, K. A., Prietula, M. J., & Cokely, E. T. (2007). The making of an expert. *Harvard Business Review*. https://hbsp.harvard.edu/product/R0707J-PDF-ENG

Eros, J. (2011). The career cycle and the second stage of teaching: Implications for policy and professional development. *Arts Education Policy Review, 112*(2), 65–70.

Farmer, R. (2001). Humanistic education and self-actualization theory. *Education, 105*(2), 162–172.

Farrell, T. S. C. (2016). TESOL, a profession that eats its young! The importance of reflective practice in language teacher education. *Iranian Journal of Language Teaching Research, 4*(3), 97–107.

Fasching-Varner, K. (2013). *Working through whiteness: Examining white racial identity and profession with pre-service teachers*. Lexington.

Feiman-Nemser, S. (2001). From preparation to practice: Designing a continuum to strengthen and sustain teaching. *Teachers College Record, 103*(6), 1013–1055. https://www.brandeis.edu/mandel/questcase/Documents/Readings/Feiman_Nemser.pdf

Felkey, A., Dziadula, E., Chiang, E. P., and Vazquez, J. (2021). Microcommitments: The effect of small commitments on student success. *AEA Papers and Proceedings, 111*, 92–96. https://doi.org/10.1257/pandp.20211043

Fessler, R., & Christensen, J. (1992). *Teacher career cycle: Understanding and guiding the professional development of teachers*. Allyn & Bacon.

Finkelstein, L. M., Ryan, K. M., & King, E. B. (2013). What do the young (old) people think of me? Content and accuracy of age-based metastereotypes. *European Journal of Work and Organizational Psychology, 22*(6), 633–657. https://doi.org/10.1080/1359432x.2012.673279

Fray, L., & Gore, J. (2018). Why people choose teaching: A scoping review of empirical studies, 2007–2016. *Teaching and Teacher Education, 75*, 153–163. https://doi.org/10.1016/j.tate.2018.06.009

Freire, P. (1970). *Pedagogy of the oppressed*. Herder and Herder.

French, K. R. (2018). First-year influences and belief adaptation: A case study of urban schoolteachers. *New Waves Educational Research & Development, 21*(1), 1–29. https://files.eric.ed.gov/fulltext/EJ1211314.pdf

Gardiner, W., Hinman, T., Tondreau, Degener, S., Dussling, T., Stevens, E. Y., Wilson, N. S., & White, K. (2022). When "nice" isn't: Confronting niceness and whiteness to center equity in teacher education. *Action in Teacher Education, 45*(2), 1–17. https://doi.org/10.1080/01626620.2022.2158390

Gavish, B., & Friedman, I. A. (2010). Novice teachers' experience of teaching: A dynamic aspect of burnout. *Social Psychology of Education, 13*, 141–167. https://doi.org/10.1007/s11218-009-9108-0

Gay, G. (2010). *Culturally responsive teaching: Theory, research and practice*. Teachers College Press.

Gay, G. (2014). Culturally responsive teaching principles, practices, and effects. In H. R. Milner & K. Lomotey (Eds.), *Handbook of urban education* (pp. 353–372). Routledge.

Giboney Wall, C. R. (2016). From student to teacher: Changes in preservice teacher educational beliefs throughout the learning-to-teach journey. *Teacher Development, 20*(3), 364–379. http://dx.doi.org/10.1080/13664530.2016.1149509

Gibson, J. (2019). Mindfulness, interoception, and the body: A contemporary perspective. *Frontiers in Psychology, 10*. https://doi.org/10.3389/fpsyg.2019.02012

Gilad, E., & Alkalay, A. (2014). The gap between role expectations of new teachers and school reality. *International Journal of Education and*

References

Research, 2(12), 473–486. http://www.ijern.com/journal/2014/December -2014/40.pdf

Gill, E. A. (2002). The impact of generational differences on teacher job satisfaction and perceptions of principal leadership. (Doctoral dissertation, Barker University). https://www.bakeru.edu/images/pdf/SOE/EdD_Theses /Gill_Emily.pdf

Glutsch, N., & König, J. (2019). Pre-service teachers' motivations for choosing teaching as a career: Does subject interest matter? *Journal of Education for Teaching, 45*(5), 494–510. https://doi.org/10.1080/02607476 .2019.1674560

Grissom, J. A., Kalogrides, D., & Loeb, S. (2015). The micropolitics of educational inequality: The case of teacher–student assignments. *Peabody Journal of Education, 90*(5), 601–614. https://doi.org/10.1080/0161956x .2015.1087768

Gu, Q., & Day, C. (2007). Teachers' resilience: A necessary condition for effectiveness. *Teaching and Teacher Education, 23*(8), 1302–1316. https:// doi.org/10.1016/j.tate.2006.06.006

Hanushek, E. A., Kain, J. F., & Rivkin, S. G. (1998). Teachers, schools, and academic achievement (August 1998). *NBER Working Paper No. w6691.* https://ssrn.com/abstract=122569

Hardy, D. (2012). *The compound effect: Jumpstart your income, your life, your success.* Hachette.

Hargreaves, H. (2005). Educational change takes ages: Life, career, and generational factors in teachers' emotional responses to educational change. *Teaching and Teacher Education, 21*(8), 967–983. https://doi.org/10 .1016/j.tate.2005.06.007

Harris, B. (2021). *17 things resilient teachers do: And 4 things they hardly ever do.* Routledge.

Headden, S. (2014). Beginners in the classroom: What the changing demographics of teaching mean for schools, students, and society. Carnegie Foundation for the Advancement of Teaching. https://www.carnegiefoundation.org /wp-content/uploads/2014/09/beginners_in_classroom.pdf

Helms, J. E. (Ed.). (1990). *Black and white racial identity: Theory, research, and practice.* Greenwood Press.

Hennessy, J., & Lynch, R. (2016). "I chose to become a teacher because." Exploring the factors influencing teaching choice amongst pre-service teachers in Ireland. *Asia-Pacific Journal of Teacher Education, 45*(2), 106–125. https://doi.org/10.1080/1359866x.2016.1183188

Herrera, S. G. (2022). *Biography-driven culturally responsive teaching: Honoring race, ethnicity, and personal history.* Teachers College Press.

Herrera, S. G., Porter, L., & Barko-Alva, K. (2020). *Equity in school-parent partnerships.* Teachers College Press.

Heubeck, E. (2021, May 5). Mentors matter for new teachers: Advice of what works and doesn't. *Education Week.* https://www.edweek.org

/leadership/mentors-matter-for-new-teachers-advice-on-what-works
-and-doesnt/2021/05

Hewett, V. (2019). *Making it as a teacher: How to survive and thrive in the first five years*. Routledge.

Hong, J., Day, C., & Greene, B. (2018). The construction of early career teachers' identities: Coping or managing? *Teacher Development, 22*(2), 249–266. https://doi.org/10.1080/13664530.2017.1403367

hooks, bell (1994). *Teaching to transgress: Education as the practice of freedom*. Routledge.

Housel, M. (2017). *The freakishly strong base*. https://collabfund.com/blog/the-freakishly-strong-base

Howard, S., & Johnson, B. (2004). Resilient teachers: Resisting stress and burnout. *Social Psychology of Education, 7*(4), 399–420. https://doi.org/10.1007/s11218-004-0975-0

Huberman, A. M. (1993). *The lives of teachers*. Teachers College Press.

Huisman, S., Singer, N. R., & Catapano, S. (2010). Resiliency to success: Supporting novice urban teachers. *Teacher Development, 14*(4), 483–499. https://doi.org/10.1080/13664530.2010.533490

Howard, G. R. (2007). Dispositions for good teaching. *Journal of Educational Controversy, 2*(2), 2. https://cedar.wwu.edu/jec/vol2/iss2/2

Htang, L. K. (2019). Motivations for choosing teaching as a career: Teacher trainees' perspective from a Myanmar context. *Journal of Education for Teaching, 45*(5), 511–524. https://doi.org/10.1080/02607476.2019.1674561

Ingersoll, R., May, H., & Collins, G. (2019). Recruitment, employment, retention and the minority teacher shortage. *Education Policy Analysis Archives, 27*(37). http://dx.doi.org/10.14507/epaa.27.3714

Ingersoll, R. M., & Smith, T. M. (2003). The wrong solution to the teacher shortage. *Educational Leadership, 60*(8), 30–33. https://www.gse.upenn.edu/pdf/rmi/EL_TheWrongSolution_to_theTeacherShortage.pdf

Jeffrey, S. (2023). *The ultimate list of core values*. https://scottjeffrey.com/core-values-list/

Jennings, P. A. (2015). *Mindfulness for teachers: Simple skills for peace and productivity in the classroom*. Norton.

Jennings, P. A. (2020). *Teacher burnout turnaround: Strategies for empowered educators*. Norton.

Johnson, B., Down, B., Le Cornu, R., Peters, J., Sullivan, A., Pearce, J., & Hunter, J. (2014). *Early career teachers*. Springer Link.

Johnson, S. M. (2019). *Where teachers thrive: Organizing schools for success*. Harvard Education Press.

Johnson, S. M., Kraft, M. A., & Papay, J. P. (2012). How context matters in high-need schools: The effects of teachers' working conditions on their professional satisfaction and their students' achievement. *Teachers College Record, 114*(10), 1–39.

References

Jones, J. M. (2021). The dual pandemics of COVID-19 and systemic racism: Navigating our path forward. *School Psychology, 36*(5), 427–431. https://doi.org/10.1037/spq0000472

Kaden, U., Patterson, P. P., Healy, J., & Adams, B. L. (2016). Stemming the revolving door: Teacher retention and attrition in Arctic Alaska schools. *Global Education Review, 3*(1), 129–147. https://files.eric.ed.gov/fulltext/EJ1090201.pdf

Kamenetz, A. (2022, February 2). More than half of teachers are looking for the exits, a poll says. *KQED.* https://www.kqed.org/mindshift/59018/more-than-half-of-teachers-are-looking-for-the-exits-a-poll-says

Kavanagh, K. M., Thacker, E. S., Williams, M. C., Merritt, J. D., Bodle, A., & Jafee, A. T. (2021). Disrupting microaggressions in P–16 classrooms: A facilitated workshop approach using critical case analysis. *Multicultural Perspectives, 23*(4), 232–240. https://doi.org/10.1080/15210960.2021.1979403

Keith, M. G., & Jagacinski, C. M. (2023). Tell me what to do, not how to do it: Influence of creative outcome and process goals on creativity. *The Journal of Creative Behavior, 57*(2), 285–304. https://doi-org.coloradocollege.idm.oclc.org/10.1002/jocb.577

Kelchtermans, G. (2017). Should I stay or should I go: Unpacking teacher attrition/retention as an educational issue. *Teachers and Teaching, 23*(8), 961–977. https://doi.org/10.1080/13540602.2017.1379793

Khatib, M., Sarem, S. N., & Hamidi, H. (2013). Humanistic education: Concerns, implications, and applications. *Journal of Language Teaching and Research, 4*(1), 45–51. https://doi.org/10.4304/jltr.4.1.45-51

Kralovec, E., Johnston, M., Mehl, W., Rickel, J., Barrington, J., Encinas, G., Ortiz, K., & Duffy, C. (2021). The value of a teacher's life. *Schools, 18*(1), 69–85. https://doi.org/10.1086/713612

LaBelle, J., & Belknap, G. (2016, January 1). *Reflective journaling: Fostering dispositional development in preservice teachers.* College of Education Faculty Research and Publications. https://core.ac.uk/download/pdf/213078954.pdf

Ladson-Billings, G. (1995). Toward a theory of culturally relevant pedagogy. *American Education Research Journal, 32*(3), 465–491.

Langshur, E., & Klemp, N. (2016). *Start here: Master the lifelong habit of wellbeing.* Gallery Books.

Lantieri, L. (2001). *Schools with spirit: Nurturing the inner lives of students and teachers.* Beacon Press.

Lee, S. W. (2018). Pulling back the curtain: Revealing the cumulative importance of high-performing, highly qualified teachers on students' educational outcome. *Educational Evaluation and Policy Analysis, 40*(3), 359–381. https://doi.org/10.3102/01623737187693797

Leonardo, Z. (2009). *Race, whiteness, and education.* Routledge.

Lewis, S., & Holloway, J. (2019). Datafying the teaching "profession": Remaking the professional teacher in the image of data. *Cambridge Journal of Education, 49*(1), 35–51. https://doi.org/10.1080/0305764X.2018.14 41373

Ley, D. (2022, April 4). Teachers are done. No, really. *Age of awareness.* https://medium.com/age-of-awareness/teachers-are-done-no-really -def0ff5d8d31

Lieberman, C. (2018). How self-care became so much work. *Harvard Business Review.* https://hbr.org/2018/08/how-self-care-became-so-much-work

Lim, C. P., & Chai, C. S. (2008). Teachers' pedagogical beliefs and their planning and conduct of computer-mediated classroom lessons. *British Journal of Educational Technology, 39*(5), 807–828. https://doi.org/10 .1111/j.1467-8535.2007.00774.x

LiquidPlanner. (2022). *How to create a personal mission and vision statement for the year.* https://www.liquidplanner.com/blog/create-personal -mission-vision-statement-year/

Locke, E. A., & Latham, G. P. (2002). Building a practically useful theory of goal setting and task motivation: A 35-year odyssey. *American Psychologist, 57*(9), 705–717. https://doi.org/10.1037/0003-066X.57.9.705

Locke, E. A., Shaw, K. N., Saari, L. M., & Latham, G. P. (1981). Goal setting and task performance: 1969–1980. *Psychological Bulletin, 90*(1), 125–152. https://doi.org/10.1037/0033-2909.90.1.125

Lohbeck, A., & Frenzel, A. C. (2021). Latent motivation profiles for choosing teaching as a career: How are they linked to self-concept concerning teaching subjects and emotions during teacher education training? *British Journal of Educational Psychology, 92*(1), 37–58. https://doi.org/10 .1111/bjep.12437

Lombardo, C. (2019, January 9). Virginia study finds increased school bullying in areas that voted for Trump. *NPR.* https://www.npr.org/2019/01 /09/683177489/virginia-study-finds-increased-school-bullying-in-areas -that-voted-for-trump

Lorde, A. (1998). *A burst of light.* Firebrand.

Love, B. L. (2020). *We want to do more than survive: Abolitionist teaching and the pursuit of academic freedom.* Beacon.

Lyons, S. T., Schweitzer, L., & Ng, E. S. W. (2015). How have careers changed? An investigation of changing career patterns across four generations. *Journal of Managerial Psychology, 30*(1), 8–21. https://doi.org /10.1108/jmp-07-2014-0210

Mahatmya, D., Grooms, A. A., Kim, J. Y., McGinnis, D. A., & Johnson, E. (2021). Burnout and race-related stress among BIPOC women K–12 educators. *Journal of Education Human Resources, 40*(1), 58–89. https:// doi.org/10.3138/jehr-2021-0007

Malcolm X Quotes. (n.d.). BrainyQuote.com. https://www.brainyquote.com /quotes/malcolm_x_386475

References

Mamiya, P. C., Richards, T., Corrigan, N. M., & Kuhl, P. K. et al. (2020). Strength of ventral tegmental area connections with left caudate nucleus is related to conflict monitoring. *Frontiers in Psychology, 10*, 1–10. https://doi.org/10.3389/fpsyg.2019.02869

Marcionetti, J., & Castelli, L. (2022). Validation of a teacher self-efficacy scale in Italian and relations with relationships with colleagues, school leadership, school innovativeness, teacher autonomy, role clarity and role conflicts. *TPM, 29*(3), 281–295. https://www.tpmap.org/wp-content/uploads/2022/09/29.3.1.pdf

Marshall, D. T., Shannon, D. M., & Love, S. M. (2020). How teachers experienced the COVID-19 transition to remote instruction. *Phi Delta Kappan, 102*(3), 46–50. https://journals.sagepub.com/doi/10.1177/0031721720970702

Maruli, S. (2014). Quality in teaching: A review of literature. *International Journal of Education and Research, 2*(12), 193–200. https://www.ijern.com/journal/2014/December-2014/18.pdf

Maslach, C., & Leiter, M. P. (2016). Understanding the burnout experience: Recent research and its implications for psychiatry. *World Psychology, 15*(2), 101–111. https://doi.org/10.1002/wps.20311

Maslow, A. H. (1943). A theory of human motivation. *Psychological Review, 50*(4), 370–396. https://doi.org/10.1037/h0054346

Maslow, A. H. (1968). Some educational implications of the humanistic psychologies. *Harvard Educational Review, 38*(4), 685–696. https://doi.org/10.17763/haer.38.4.j07288786v86w660

Maslow, A. H. (1972). *The farther reaches of human nature*. Viking Press.

McChesney, K., & Aldridge, J. M. (2019). A review of practitioner-led evaluation of teacher professional development. *Professional Development in Education, 45*(2), 307–324. https://doi.org/10.1080/19415257.2018.1452782

McLean, L., Abry, T., Taylor, M., & Gaias, L. (2020). The influence of adverse classroom and school experiences on first year teachers' mental health and career optimism. *Teaching and Teacher Education, 87*, 1–13. https://doi.org/10.1016/j.tate.2019.102956

McMahon, M., Forde, C., & Dickson, B. (2015). Reshaping teacher education through the professional continuum. *Educational Review, 67*(2), 158–178. https://doi.org/10.1080/00131911.2013.846298

McTighe, J., & Wiggins, G. P. (2005). *Understanding by design: Professional development workbook*. Association for Supervision and Curriculum Development.

Menakem, R. (2017). *My grandmother's hands: Racialized trauma and the pathway to mending our hearts and bodies*. Central Recovery Press.

Mills, J., Wand, T., & Fraser, J. A. (2018). Examining self-care, self-compassion, and compassion for others: A cross-sectional survey of palliative care nurses and doctors. *International Journal of Palliative*

Nursing, 24(1), 4–11. https://eprints.qut.edu.au/223452/1/115747.pdf

Mitchell, L. S. (2008). Growth of teachers in professional maturity. In M. Cochran-Smith, S. Feiman-Nemser, D. J. McIntyre, & K. E. Demers (Eds.), *Handbook of research on teacher education: Enduring questions in changing contexts* (3rd ed., pp. 800–807). Routledge.

Mobra, T. J., & Hamlin, D. E. (2020). Emergency certified teachers' motivations for entering the teaching profession: Evidence from Oklahoma. *Education Policy Analysis Archives, 28*, 109. https://doi.org/10.14507/epaa.28.5295

Moir, E. (1990). Phases of first-year teaching. *California New Teacher Project*. https://www.jefferson.kyschools.us/sites/default/files/Phases%20of%20First%20Year%20Teachers.pdf

Molero-Jurado, M. D, Pérez-Fuentez, M. D., Atria, L., Ruiz, N. F., & Lindares, J. J. (2019). Burnout, perceived efficacy, and job satisfaction: Perception of the education context in high school teachers. *Biomed Research International,* 2019, 1–11. https://doi.org/10.1155/2019/1021408

Montero-Marin, J., Taylor, L., Crane, C., Greenberg, M. T., Ford, T. J., Williams, J. M. G., García-Campayo, J., Sonley, A., Lord, L., Dalgleish, T., Blakemore, S.-J., MYRIAD team, & Kuyken, W. (2021). Teachers "finding peace in a frantic world": An experimental study of self-taught and instructor-led mindfulness program formats on acceptability, effectiveness, and mechanisms. *Journal of Educational Psychology, 113*(8), 1689–1708. https://doi.org/10.1037/edu0000542

Msila, V. (2019). Conflict management and transformation's impact on school progress: A case study of two schools. *The International Journal of Educational Organization and Leadership, 26*(2), 57–71. https://doi.org/10.18848/2329-2656/cgp/v26i02/57-71

Munroe, A. M. (2022). Novice and experienced music teacher resilience: A comparative case study. *Research Studies in Music Education, 44*(1), 99–109. https://journals.sagepub.com/doi/pdf/10.1177/1321103X211023248

Nagoski, E., & Nagoski, A. (2019). *Burnout: The secret to unlocking the stress cycle*. Ballantine.

National Center for Education Statistics (NCES). (2019). *Status and trends in the education of racial and ethnic groups 2018*. https://nces.ed.gov/pubs2019/2019038.pdf

National Center for Education Statistics. (2021). *Digest of education statistics: 2019* (NCES 2021-009). https://nces.ed.gov/programs/digest/d19/foreword.asp

National Education Association (NEA). (2022, January). *Poll results: Stress and burnout pose threat of educator shortages.* https://www.nea.org/sites/default/files/2022-02/NEA%20Member%20COVID-19%20Survey%20Summary.pdf

References

Nguyen, T. D., & Springer, M. G. (2021). A conceptual framework of teacher turnover: A systematic review of the empirical international literature and insights from the employee turnover literature. *Educational Review,* 75(5), 993–1028. https://doi.org/10.1080/00131911.2021.1940103

Nichols, S. L., Schutz, P. A., Rodgers, K., & Bilica, K. (2016). Early career teachers' emotion and emerging teacher identities. *Teachers and Teaching: Theory and Practice, 23*(4), 406–421. https://doi.org/10.1080/1354 0602.2016.1211099

Nieto, S. (Ed.). (2005). *Why we teach.* Teachers College Press.

Nieto, S. (2013). *Finding joy in teaching students of diverse backgrounds: Culturally responsive and socially just practices in U.S. classrooms.* Heineman.

Noddings, N. (2005). *The challenge to care in schools: An alternative approach to education.* Teachers College Press.

Nordell, B. B. (2021). *Avoiding burnout: How exemplary teachers find fuel and cultivate success.* Rowman & Littlefield.

Palmer, P. J. (2017). *The courage to teach: Exploring the inner landscape of a teacher's life* (3rd ed.). Jossey-Bass.

Pantić, N., Galey, S., Florian, L., Joksimović, S., Viry, G., Gašević, D., Knutes Nyqvist, H., & Kyritsi, K. (2022). Making sense of teacher agency for change with social and epistemic network analysis. *Journal of Educational Change, 23*(2), 145–177. https://doi.org/10.1007/s10833-021 -09413-7

Papay, J., Bacher-Hicks, A., Page, L., & Marinell, W. (2015). The challenge of teacher retention in urban schools: Using evidence from 16 districts in 7 states to examine variation across sites. *Association for Public Policy Analysis and Management Big Data and Public Policy Workshop*, Miami, FL. *Educational Researcher, 46*(8),434–448. http://dx.doi.org/10 .3102/0013189X17735812

Paris, D., & Alim, H. S. (Eds.). (2017). *Culturally sustaining pedagogies: Teaching and learning for justice in a changing world.* Teachers College Press.

Perrone, F., Player, D., & Youngs, P. (2019). Administrative climate, early career teacher burnout, and turnover. *Journal of School Leadership, 29*(3), 191–209. https://doi.org/10.1177/1052684619836823

Powell, R., & Rightmyer, E. (Eds.). (2011). *Literacy for all students: An instructional framework for closing the gap.* Routledge.

Psychology Today. (2023). Mindfulness. https://www.psychologytoday.com /us/basics/mindfulness

Räsänen, K., Pietarinen, J., Pyhältö, K., Soini, T., & Väisänen, K. (2020). Why leave the teaching profession? A longitudinal approach to the prevalence and persistence of teacher turnover intentions. *Social Psychology of Education, 23*, 837–859. https://doi.org/10.1007/s11218 -020-09567-x

Reichenberg, J. S. (2022). Teacher agency as a route to adaptive expertise: Relational, informed, and reflective action. *Reading Horizons, 61*(2), 65–85.

Rios, F., & Longoria, A. (2021). *Creating a home in schools: Sustaining identities for Black, Indigenous and teachers of color.* Teachers College Press.

Ro, J. (2019). Learning to teach in the era of test-based accountability: A review of research. *Professional Development in Education, 45*(1), 87–101. https://doi.org/10.1080/19415257.2018.1514525

Romero, G. (2021). Deconstructing novice teachers' actions and reactions to nonharmonic Chilean school communities of practice. *Issues From Teacher Researchers, 23*(1), 13–26. https://doi.org/10.15446/profile.v23 n1.83955

Ryken, A. E., & Hamel, F. L. (2016). Looking again at "surface-level" reflections: Framing a competence view of early teacher thinking. *Teacher Education Quarterly, 43*(4), 31–53. http://www.worldcat.org /oclc/6870890675

Saint Francis de Sales Quotes. (n.d.). BrainyQuote.com. https://www .brainyquote.com/quotes/saint_francis_de_sales_193306

Santoro, D. A. (2018). *Demoralized: Why teachers leave the profession they love and how they can stay.* Harvard Education Press.

Saviuc, L. D. (n.d.). *Maya Angelou: 21 life-changing lessons to learn from the loving Maya Angelou.* https://www.purposefairy.com/70194/life-les sons-maya-angelou

Schaefer, L. (2013). Beginning teacher attrition: A question of identity making and identity shifting. *Teachers and Teaching: Theory and Practice, 19*(3), 260–274. https://doi.org/10.1080/13540602.2012.754159

Schaefer, L., & Clandinin, D. J. (2018). Sustaining teachers' stories to live by: Implications for teacher education. *Teachers and Teaching: Theory and Practice, 25*(1), 54–68. https://doi.org/10.1080/13540602.2018.1532407

Schutz, P., Hong, J. Y., & Francis, D. C. (Eds.). (2019). *Research on teacher identity: Mapping challenges and innovations.* Springer Nature.

Scott, S. (2017). *Fierce conversations: Achieving success at work and in life, one conversation at a time.* New American Library.

Shedrow, S. (2021). Student engagement and digital tools: Lessons learned during the COVID-19 pandemic. *AILACTE Journal, 18*, 1–26. https:// ailacte.org/images/downloads/ailacte21_for_web_apr1.pdf

Shirazizadeh, M., & Karimpour, M. (2019). An investigation of the relationships among EFL teachers' perfectionism, reflection, and burnout. *Cogent Education, 6*(1), 1–13. https://doi.org/10.1080/2331186X.2019.16 67708

Southern Regional Education Board (SREB). (2018). Mentoring new teachers: A fresh look. *Educator Effectiveness.* https://www.sreb.org/mentoring

References

Starr, R. W. (2018). Moving from the mainstream to the margins: Lessons in culture and power. *Journal of Family Violence, 33,* 551–557. https://doi.org/10.1007/s10896-018-9984-1

Steffy, B., Wolfe, M., Pasch, S., & Enz, B. (Eds.). (2000). *Life cycle of the career teacher.* Corwin Press.

Sue, D. W. (2015). *Race talk and the conspiracy of silence: Understanding and facilitating difficult dialogues on race.* John Wiley & Sons.

Sulis, G., Babic, S., Mairitsch, A., Mercer, S., Jin, J., & King, J. (2022). Retention and attrition in early-career foreign language teachers in Austria and the United Kingdom. *The Modern Language Journal.* https://onlinelibrary.wiley.com/doi/pdf/10.1111/modl.12765

Sunthonkanokpong, W., & Murphy, E. (2019). Quality, equity, inclusion, and lifelong learning in pre-service teacher education. *Journal of Teacher Education for Sustainability, 21*(2), 91–104. https://doi.org/10.2478/jtes-2019-0019

Sutcher, L., Darling-Hammond, L., & Carver-Thomas, D. (2016). A coming crisis in teaching? Teacher supply, demand, and shortages in the U.S. Learning Policy Institute. https://doi.org/10.54300/247.242

Tait, M. (2008). Resilience as a contributor to novice teacher success, commitment, and retention. *Teacher Education Quarterly, 35*(4), 57–75. https://www.jstor.org/stable/23479174

Tamir, E. (2013). Choosing teaching as a career in urban public Catholic and Jewish schools by graduates of elite colleges. *Journal of Educational Change, 15*(3), 327–355. https://doi.org/10.1007/s10833-013-9222-9

Tang, Y., Posner, M., & Holzel, B. (2015). The neuroscience of mindfulness meditation. *Nature Reviews Neuroscience, 16,* 213–225. https://doi.org/10.1007/978-3-319-46322-3

TeKippe, S. S., Bechtel, M., Faga, K. K., & Szabo, M. R. (2020). The 3CM approach: A pedagogy based on theory and experience to move beyond the "what" into the "how" toward a pathway of lifelong learning and teaching. *International Journal of Pedagogy & Curriculum, 27*(1), 39–52. https://doi.org/10.18848/2327-7963/CGP/v27i01/39-52

Thomas, K., & Kilman, R. (1978). Comparison of four instruments measuring conflict behavior. *Psychological Reports, 42*(3), 1139–1145. https://kilmanndiagnostics.com/wp-content/uploads/2018/05/Thomas-Kilmann-Four-Instruments.pdf https://doi.org/10.2466/pr0.1978.42.3c.11

Ticknor, A. S. (2014). Negotiating professional identities in teacher education: A closer look at the language of one preservice teacher. *The New Educator, 10*(4), 289–305. https://doi.org/10.1080/1547688x.2014.965094

Trevethan, H. (2018). Challenging the discourse of beginning teaching: Only one crying phone call. *New Zealand Journal of Educational Studies, 53*(1), 49–63. http://dx.doi.org/10.1007/s40841-018-0105-8

Truscott, D., & Barker, K. S. (2020). Developing teacher identities as in situ teacher educators through communities of practice. *The New Educator, 16*(4), 333–351. https://doi.org/10.1080/1547688x.2020.1779890

Ulferts, J. D. (2016, March). Won't you stay a little longer? The challenge in rural America of teacher recruitment and retention. *The Superintendents Association.* https://www.aasa.org/resources/resource/wont-you-stay-little-longer

UNESCO. (2016a). *Education 2030: Incheon declaration and framework for action for the implementation of sustainable development goal 4.* 1–83. https://uis.unesco.org/sites/default/files/documents/education-2030-incheon-framework-for-action-implementation-of-sdg4-2016-en_2.pdf

U.S. Department of Education Office of Postsecondary Education. (2017). *Teacher shortage areas nationwide listings 1990–1991 through 2017–18.* U.S. Department of Education. https://www2.ed.gov/about/offices/list/ope/pol/ateachershortageareasreport2017-18.pdf

Vacca, R. T., Mraz, M. E., & Vacca, J. A. L. (2021). *Content area reading: Literacy and learning across the curriculum.* Pearson.

Valtierra, K. M. (2016). Beyond survival to thrival: An Urban Teacher's Promising Career Story. *Curriculum and Teaching Dialogue, 18*(1–2), 55–69. https://www.infoagepub.com/products/Curriculum-and-Teaching-Dialogue-Vol-18

Valtierra, K. M. (2022). Teach and thrive learning circles: Priming early career teachers to flourish. *AILACTE Journal, 16,* 109–135. https://files.eric.ed.gov/fulltext/EJ1381643.pdf

Valtierra, K. M. (2023). Navigating structural disillusionment through relational persistence: How ten early career teachers remained committed to urban teaching. *American Education Research Association* (AERA). Chicago, Illinois.

Valtierra, K. M., & Michalec, P. (2017). Deep curriculum: Guiding the inner lives of early career teachers. *Curriculum and Teaching Dialogue, 19*(1–2), 19–33.

Valtierra, K. M., & Siegel, L. N. (2022). Qualitative coding as a pedagogy for fostering dispositions and reflexivity. *The Qualitative Report, 27*(1), 257–267. https://nsuworks.nova.edu/tqr/vol27/iss1/18/

Valtierra, K. M., & Whitaker, M. C. (2021). Beliefs or classroom context: What matters most to novice urban teachers' enactment of culturally responsive pedagogy? *The Urban Review: Issues and Ideas in Public Education, 53*(5), 857–880. https://doi.org/10.1007/s11256-021-00599-x

van Lankveld, T., Schoonenboom, J., Volman, M., Croiset, G., & Beishuizen, J. (2017). Developing a teacher identity in the university context: A systematic review of the literature. *Higher Education Research & Development, 36*(2), 325–342. https://doi.org/10.1080/07294360.2016.1208154

References

Vilar, J., Riberas, G., & Rosa, G. (2016). How social educators manage conflicts of values. *Ramon Llull Journal of Applied Ethics, 7*(7), 207–230. https://raco.cat/index.php/rljae/article/view/310549

Watt, H. M., & Richardson, P. W. (2007). Motivational factors influencing teaching as a career choice: Development and validation of the FIT-choice scale. *The Journal of Experimental Education, 75*(3), 167–202. https://doi.org/10.3200/jexe.75.3.167-202

Watt, H. M. G., & Richardson, P. W. (2012). An introduction to teaching motivations in different countries: Comparisons using the FIT-choice scale. *Asia-Pacific Journal of Teacher Education, 40*(3), 185–197. https://doi.org/10.1080/1359866x.2012.700049

Weiner, J. M. (2020). From new to nuanced: (Re)Considering educator professionalism and its impacts. *Journal of Educational Change, 21*, 443–454. https://doi.org/10.1007/s10833-020-09371-6

Whitaker, M. C., & Valtierra, K. M. (2019). *Schooling multicultural teachers.* Emerald.

Will, M. (2022, April 15). Disrespected and dissatisfied: 7 takeaways from new survey of teachers. *Education Week.* https://www.edweek.org/teaching-learning/disrespected-and-dissatisfied-7-takeaways-from-a-new-survey-of-teachers/2022/04

Wong, H. K., & Wong, R. T. (2018). *The classroom management book* (2nd ed.). Harry K. Wong Publications.

Wronowski, M. L. (2020). De-professionalized and demoralized: A framework for understanding teacher turnover in the accountability policy ERA. *Leadership and Policy in Schools, 20*(4), 599–629. https://doi.org/10.1080/15700763.2020.1734209

Wu, J., Smith, S., Khurana, M., Siemaszko, C., & DeJesus-Banos, B. (2020). Stay-at home orders across the country: What each state is doing—or not doing—amid widespread coronavirus lockdowns. *NBC News.* https://www.nbcnews.com/health/health-news/here-are-stay-homeorders-across-country-n1168736

Yadav, R. S., Dash, S. S., Sinha, S., & Palky, J. (2020). Impact of work-place bullying on turnover intention: A study among Indian school teachers. *South Asian Journal of Management, 27*(4), 33–58.

Yakavets, N., Winter, L., Malone, K., Zhontayeva, Z., & Khamidulina, Z. (2022). Educational reform and teachers' agency in reconstructing pedagogical practices in Kazakhstan. *Journal of Educational Change, 24*, 1–31. https://doi.org/10.1007/s10833-022-09463-5

Zaharis, M. (2019). High-quality teacher induction and multi-year mentoring: Are the new teachers in your school thriving or merely surviving? *Lutheran Education, 155*(4), 1–6.

Zeichner, K. (2022). Preparing teachers to teach successfully in schools in historically marginalized communities. *Márgenes, Revista de Educación de la Universidad de Málaga, 3*(3), 83–97. http://dx.doi.org/10.24310/mgnmar.v3i3.15343

Zolkoski, S. M., & Lewis-Chiu, C. (2019). Alternative approaches: Implementing mindfulness practices in the classroom to improve challenging behaviors. *Beyond Behavior, 28*(1), 46–54. https://doi.org/10.1177/1074295619832943

Index

Abry, T., 80, 81, 83
Academic protocol, 68
Activate, Connect, Affirm (A-C-A), 36
Adams, B. L., 16
Adams, N. E., 94
Aguilar, E., 89
Ainsworth, S., 19
Aldridge, J. M., 24
Alifah, P., 9
Alim, H. S., 4, 9
Alkalay, A., 3
Allen, J., 9
Allies, S., 16, 23, 79, 80, 82, 83
Alsup, J., 20
Altruistic motivations, 29–32, 43
Alvarinas-Villaverde, M., 30
American Psychological Association
 (APA), 79, 80
Anderson, D., 81
Anderson, L., 3
Angelou, M., 92
Arch, D. A. N., 80
Atatürk, M. K., 109
Atomic Habits: An Easy and Proven
 Way to Build Good Habits and
 Break Bad Ones, 95
Atria, L., 17
Aubusson, P., 63–64
Austin, J. R., 21
Authentic teacher identity
 commitment to praxis, 42–43
 forming true relationships, 27
 preservice and early career teachers,
  41–43
 psychological motivations, 30–31

purpose and identity, 31–32
purpose under pressure, 27–29
Summer's personalized planning
 template, 38–40
Summer's umbrella goals, 36, 37
support novice teachers, 32–34
Theory to Practice Project, 35–41
TTLC participants, 42
Au, W., 3, 76

Babauta, L., 96
Babic, S., 3, 19, 21, 23
Bacher-Hicks, A., 16, 109
Baliram, N., 15
Ball, S. J., 16
Bandura, A., 94
Banks, J., 4, 9
Barkatsas, A., 80
Barker, K. S., 20
Barko-Alva, K., 64
Barrington, J., 78, 80
Bechtel, M., 81
Before, During, and After (B-D-A)
 method, 36
Beijaard, D., 24
Beishuizen, J., 19
Belknap, G., 85
Bergh, B., 81
Bieler, D., 81
Biesta, G., 19
Bilica, K., 19
Biography-Driven Culturally
 Responsive Teaching, 36
Blakemore, S.-J., 82, 83
Bodle, A., 68, 76

Bohjanen, S., 81
Bonilla-Silva, E., 67
Boogren, T., 81–84, 86, 89
Bressman, S., 46, 47
Brown, B., 61, 71, 97
Buchanan, J., 63–64
Burke, P., 63–64

Cabrera, C. M., 66
Cameron-Standerford, A., 81
Carver-Thomas, D., 14
Castelli, L., 64
Castro, A. J., 21
Catapano, S., 21
Chai, C. S., 81
Chiang, E. P., 94, 95
Christensen, J., 46–47, 51
Clandinin, D. J., 20, 24, 31, 68
Clark, S. K., 80, 83
The Classroom Management Book, 36
Clear, J., 83, 84, 94–97, 99
Cobb, D. J., 22
Cohen, R. M., 76
Cokely, E. T., 80
Colorblind protocol, 67–68
Conflict at school
  academic protocol, 68
  beliefs and values, 65
  colorblind protocol, 67–68
  conflict avoidance, 66
  generational tension, 65
  job satisfaction, 64
  politeness protocol, 67
  workplace bullying, 65–66
Connelly, F. M., 68
Content Area Reading, 36
Costello, M. B., 76
The Courage to Teach, 15, 31–33
Coutler, S., 46, 47, 51
Cowie, H., 66, 74
Crain, W., 8
Crane, C., 82, 83
Croiset, G., 19
Cuban, L., 80
Culturally and linguistically diverse
  (CLD), 3, 4, 36

Culturally relevant teaching (CRT), 4
Culturally responsive pedagogy
  (CRP), 4
Culturally sustaining pedagogy (CSP), 4

Dantley, M. E., 29, 31, 32
Dare to Lead, 97
Darling-Hammond, L., 3, 13–14, 49
Dash, S. S., 66, 74
Daugherty, A. A., 79
Day, C., 19, 21–23
De Clercq, M., 81, 83
DeJesus-Banos, B., 14
Dell'Angelo, T., 49
de Sales, F., 45
Diamond, J., 3
Dicke, T., 82, 83
Dickson, B., 81
Dominguez-Alonso, J., 30
Doran, G. T., 95
Dos Santos, L. M., 30
Down, B., 20
Duchesne, S., 8
Duffy, C., 78, 80
Dunn, A. H., 3
Dussling, T., 67
Dziadula, E., 94, 95

Efron, S. E., 46, 47
Encinas, G., 78, 80
Endo, R., 8
Enz, B., 46–47, 51
Epstein, J., 64
Ericsson, K. A., 80
Eros, J., 47, 51
Extrinsic motivations, 30

Faga, K. K., 81
Farmer, R., 9
Farrell, T. S. C., 64, 65, 73
Fasching-Varner, K., 67
Feiman-Nemser, S., 47–49, 80, 81
Felkey, A., 94, 95
Fessler, R., 46–47, 51
Finkelstein, L. M., 65, 74
Florian, L., 22

Index

Forde, C., 81
Ford, T. J., 82, 83
Francis, D. C., 19, 20, 31
Fraser, J. A., 79
Fray, L., 29–30
Freire, P., 35, 43, 76
French, K. R., 49
Frenzel, A. C., 30
Friedman, I. A., 64

Gaias, L., 80, 81, 83
Galey, S., 22
Garcia-Campayo, J., 82, 83
Gardiner, W., 67
Gašević, D., 22
Gavish, B., 64
Gay, G., 9
Giboney Wall, C. R., 48, 49
Gibson, J., 69
Gilad, E., 3
Gill, E. A., 65
Glutsch, N., 30
Gore, J., 29–30
Greenberg, M. T., 82, 83
Greene, B., 19, 21, 23
Grissom, J. A., 81
Grooms, A. A., 9, 109
Gu, Q., 21

Hamel, F. L., 85
Hamidi, H., 8
Hamlin, D. E., 30
Hanushek, E. A., 13
Hardy, D., 96
Hargreaves, H., 46, 47
Harris, B., 62, 63, 73
Headden, S., 1, 3, 41, 47
Healy, J., 16
Helms, J. E., 67
Hennessy, J., 30
Herrera, S., 36, 64
Heubeck, E., 10
Hewett, V., 49
Hinman, T., 67
Holloway, J., 16
Holmes, S., 81

Holzel, B., 82
Hong, J., 19–21, 23, 31
hooks, b., 1, 76
Housel, M., 96
Howard, G., 7
Howard, S., 21
Htang, L. K., 30
Huberman, A. M., 47, 49, 51
Huff, E., 15
Huisman, S., 21
Humanistic teacher development
designing personal plans, 98–101
goals, 95–96
habits, 95
identity goals, 100, 101, 104
micro-commitments, 100, 101, 103, 106
outcome goals, 100, 104
process and benchmark goals, 100, 102, 105
SMARRT goals, 100–102, 104
systems, 95–96
uncovering teacher values, 97, 98
vision and mission statements, 98, 99
Hunter, J., 20

Ingersoll, R. M., 3, 14
Intrinsic motivations, 30, 31

Jafee, A. T., 68, 76
Jagacinski, C. M., 96
Jeffrey, S., 42, 98
Jennings, P. A., 19, 69, 79, 80, 82, 83
Jin, J., 3, 19, 21, 23
Johnson, B., 20, 21
Johnson, E., 9, 109
Johnson, S. M., 3, 23
Johnston, M., 78, 80
Joksimović, S., 22
Jones, J. M., 8

Kaden, U., 16
Kain, J. F., 13
Kalogrides, D., 81
Kamenetz, A., 8

Karimpour, M., 10
Kavanagh, K. M., 68, 76
Keith, M. G., 96
Kelchtermans, G., 47, 51
Kelly, J., 21
Khamidulina, Z., 24
Khatib, M., 8
Khurana, M., 14
Kim, J. Y., 9, 109
King, E. B., 65, 74
King, J., 3, 19, 21, 23
Klemp, N., 83
Knutes Nyqvist, H., 22
Koerner, B. D., 21
Koetje, K., 15
Konig, J., 30
Kraft, M. A., 3
Kralovec, E., 78, 80
Kunter, M., 82, 83
Kuyken, W., 82, 83
Kyritsi, K., 22

LaBelle, J., 85
Ladson-Billings, G., 4, 9
Langshur, E., 83
Lantieri, L., 29, 31, 32
Latham, G. P., 29, 95
Lawrie, S. I., 80
Le Cornu, R., 20
Lee, S. W., 13
Leiter, M. P., 17
Leonardo, Z., 67
Lester, J. N., 46, 47, 51
Leutner, D., 82, 83
Lewis-Chiu, C., 83
Lewis, S., 16
Ley, D., 8
Lieberman, C., 83
Life Cycle Model for Career Teachers, 47, 48
Lim, C. P., 81
Lindares, J. J., 17
Linninger, C., 82, 83
Locke, E. A., 29, 95
Loeb, S., 81
Lohbeck, A., 30

Lombardo, C., 76
Longoria, A., 9, 109
Lorde, A., 77
Lord, L., 82, 83
Louviere, J., 63–64
Love, B. L., 8
Love, S. M., 15
Lynch, R., 30
Lyons, S. T., 65

Mahatmya, D., 9, 109
Mairitsch, A., 3, 19, 21, 23
Malcolm X, 13
Malone, J., 80
Malone, K., 24
Marcionetti, J., 64
Marinell, W., 16, 109
Marshall, D. T., 15
Maruli, S., 13
Maslach, C., 17
McChesney, K., 24
McGinnis, D. A., 9, 109
McLean, L., 80, 81, 83
McMahon, M., 81
McMaugh, A., 8
McTighe, J., 36
Mehl, W., 78, 80
Menakem, R., 92
Mercer, S., 3, 19, 21, 23
Merritt, J. D., 68, 76
Michalec, P., 31
Mills, J., 79
Mitchell, L. S., 46, 47
Mobra, T. J., 30
Moir, E., 18, 49
Molero-Jurado, M., 17
Montero-Marin, J., 82, 83
Mraz, M. E., 36
Msila, V., 63, 73
Munroe, A. M., 21
Murphy, E., 48

Nagoski, A., 17
Nagoski, E., 17
National Education Association (NEA) study reports, 15

Index

Naylor, P., 66, 74
New York Times, 95
Ng, E. S. W., 65
Nguyen, T. D., 16, 109
Nichols, S. L., 19
Nieto, S., 20
No Child Left Behind (NCLB) reform, 2
Noddings, N., 29, 31, 32
Nordell, B. B., 64
Novice teachers
  conflict at school, 63–68
  envisioning the future reflection, 34
  naming present purpose, 32–33
  preservice and early career teachers, 68–73
  reflection on purpose, 33
  suggestions, 72–73
  tension with colleagues, 61–63
  thriving through tension, 74–76
  unearthing wisdom, 34
Nylund-Gibson, K., 80

Oldfield, J., 19
Olsen, B., 3
Onward: Cultivating Emotional Resilience in Educators, 89
Ortiz, K., 78, 80

Page, L., 16, 109
Palky, J., 66, 74
Palmer, P. J., 19–20, 27, 29, 31–34
Pantić, N., 22
Papay, J., 3, 16, 109
Paris, D., 4, 9
Pasch, S., 46–47, 51
Patterson, P. P., 16
Pearce, J., 20
Pereira, B., 66, 74
Perez-Fuentez, M. D., 17
Perrone, F., 23
Peters, J., 20
Pietarinen, J., 16
Player, D., 23
Politeness protocol, 67
Portela-Pino, I., 30

Porter, L., 64
Posner, M., 82
Powell, R., 64
Prescott, A., 63–64
Preservice and early career teachers
  building up, 91–92
  designing personal plans, 98–101
  mindfulness and stories of tension, 68–70
  productive conflict resolution, 70–73
  school-related tension and conflict, 74
  starting small, 90–91
  uncovering teacher values, 97–98
  vision and mission statements, 98, 99
  well-being teachers, 83–88
Priestley, M., 19
Prietula, M. J., 80
Professional learning communities (PLCs), 11
Pumares-Lavandeira, L., 30
Pyhalto, K., 16

Race Talk and the Conspiracy of Silence, 67
Rasanen, K., 16
Reichenberg, J. S., 24
Riberas, G., 64, 65
Richardson, P., 30, 81, 83
Rickel, J., 78, 80
Rightmyer, E., 64
Rios, F., 9, 109
Rivers, I., 66, 74
Rivkin, S. G., 13
Robinson, S., 19
Rodgers, K., 19
Ro, J., 24, 49
Romero, G., 64, 65, 73
Rosa, G., 64, 65
Ruiz, N. F., 17
Ryan, K. M., 65, 74
Ryken, A. E., 85

Saari, L. M., 95
Santoro, D. A., 17–19
Sarem, S. N., 8

Schaefer, L., 3, 20, 24, 31
Schoonenboom, J., 19
Schuck, S., 63–64
Schutz, P., 19, 20, 31
Schweitzer, L., 65
Shannon, D. M., 15
Sharkey, J. D., 80
Shaw, K. N., 95
Shedrow, S., 14
Shih, M., 21
Shirazizadeh, M., 10
Siegel, L. N., 85
Siemaszko, C., 14
Singer, N. R., 21
Sinha, S., 66, 74
Smith, P. K., 66, 74
Smith, S., 14
Smith, T. M., 3, 14
Soini, T., 16
Sonley, A., 82, 83
Spillane, J., 3
Springer, M. G., 16, 109
Starr, R. W., 9
Stebner, F., 82, 83
Steffy, B., 46–47, 51
Stevens, E. Y., 67
Sue, D. W., 67
Sulis, G., 3, 10, 19, 21, 23
Sullivan, A., 20
Sunthonkanokpong, W., 48
Supporting Teacher Wellbeing, 82
Sutcher, L., 14
Szabo, M. R., 81

Tait, M., 21, 23
Take Time for You: Self-Care Action Plans for Educators, 84–86, 89
Tamir, E., 30
Tang, Y., 82
Taylor, L., 82, 83
Taylor, M., 80, 81, 83
Teach and Thrive Learning Circles (TTLC), 3–6, 42, 74, 78
Teacher development
  apprentice phase, 52–53
  early career, 47

goals, 54–56
late career, 47
life cycle, 51
middle career, 47
novice teaching, 47–50, 52
personal reflection, 54
practicing patience, 57
preservice and early careers, 56–58
professional phase, 53
resilience, 45–46
thriving in community, 57–58
transparent lecture, 50–54
Teacher educator
  early career teachers, 10
  equitable and thriving teachers, 3–4
  humanistic learning theory, 7–9
  humanistic teacher development, 9–10
  professional learning communities (PLCs), 11
  social location and lens, 7
  TTLC workshops, 4–6
Teachers
  ability to thrive, 22–24
  agency, 21–22
  burnout, 17
  call to support, 109–111
  careers, 24, 25
  in COVID-19 pandemic, 15
  demoralization, 18–19
  disillusionment, 18
  education reform, 15–16
  identity, 19–20
  inadequate working conditions, 14
  personal attributes, 19–22
  quality teachers, 13
  recruitment and retention, 16
  resilience, 20–21
  shortages, 14
  unqualified teachers, 14
Teacher Wellbeing: A Practical Guide for Primary Teachers and School Leaders, 89
Teaching, 1, 25
Teach, Rehearse, and Reinforce (T-R-R) method, 36

Index

TeKippe, S. S., 81
Thacker, E. S., 68, 76
Ticknor, A. S., 20, 24, 31
Tondreau, D., 67
Trevethan, H., 22, 23
Truscott, D., 20

Ulferts, J. D., 16, 109
Understanding by Design (UbD)
curriculum, 36

Vacca, J. A. L., 36
Vacca, R. T., 36
Vaisanen, K., 16
Valtierra, K. M., 5, 10, 17, 18, 20, 31,
36, 47, 67, 76, 77, 81, 85
van Lankveld, T., 19
Vazquez, J., 94, 95
Vilar, J., 64, 65
Viry, G., 22
Volman, M., 19

Wand, T., 79
Watt, H. M., 30, 81, 83
Weiner, J. M., 16
Well-being teachers
being overworked, 79
check commitment, 88
connection, 84–85
day-to-day workload, 80
demand classroom environments, 81
evaluation processes, 81
humanistic teacher development, 92

job ambiguity, 81
Maslow's hierarchy, 85–86
mindfulness, 84
personal well-being, 85–87
preservice and early career teachers,
90–92
reclaims, 77–79
reflection, 85
working principles, 82–83
Where Teachers Thrive, 23
Whitaker, M. C., 36, 67, 76, 77, 81
White, K., 67
Wiggins, G. P., 36
Williams, J. M. G., 82, 83
Williams, M. C., 68, 76
Wilson, N. S., 67
Winter, J. S., 46, 47
Winter, L., 24
Wolfe, E. W., 81
Wolfe, M., 46–47, 51
Wong, H. K., 36
Wong, R. T., 36
Wronowski, M. L., 14
Wu, J., 14

Yadav, R. S., 66, 74
Yakavets, N., 24
Youngs, P., 23

Zaharis, M., 23
Zeichner, K., 64
Zhontayeva, Z., 24
Zolkoski, S. M., 83

About the Author

Kristina M. Valtierra is an associate professor and chair of education at Colorado College and the 2021–2024 Ray O. Werner Endowed Professor for Exemplary Teaching in the Liberal Arts. Dr. Valtierra spent over 15 years as a K–12 classroom teacher, instructional coach, and educational consultant. Her expertise is in literacy, curriculum, and instruction, emphasizing antiracist, diversity, equity, and inclusive (ADEI) studies. Her research examines urban teacher preparation, focusing on promoting teacher reflection, identity, and thrival. She is the author of *Teach and Thrive: Wisdom from an Urban Teachers Career Narrative*, co-author of *Schooling Multicultural Teachers: A Guide to Program Assessment and Professional Development*, and a two-time recipient of the American Association for Teaching and Curriculum (AATC) distinguished article award for her scholarship on teacher identity formation. Her courses, such as Youth Organizing for Social Change, Critical Multicultural Education, Culturally Sustaining Teaching, and Inclusive Pedagogies in Literacy, Curriculum & Instruction, inform her research and course syllabi. In her free time, she enjoys spending time in the beautiful state of Colorado with her husband, three children, and golden retriever.